BERLITZ®

COPENHAGEN

- A ✓ in the text denotes a highly recommended sight
- A complete A–Z of practical information starts on p.113
- Extensive mapping throughout: on cover flaps and in text

Printed in Switzerland by Weber SA, Bienne.

17th edition (1995/1996)

Although we make every effort to ensure the accuracy of the information in this guide, changes do occur. If you have any new information, suggestions or corrections to contribute to the guide, we would like to hear from you. Please write to Berlitz Publishing at one of the above addresses.

Text:	Vernon Leonard
Editors:	Brigitte Lee, Peter Duncan
Photography:	Jon Davison
Layout:	Suzanna Boyle
Cartography:	Visual Image
Thanks to:	Wonderful Copenhagen and the Danish Tourist Board for their invaluable help in the preparation of this guide.

Front cover: *Nyhavn, Copenhagen*
Back cover: *Danish cannon*
p. 4 photograph: *Tivoli Gardens, Copenhagen*

CONTENTS

Copenhagen and the Danes

In spite of its compact size, Denmark has more than its fair share of attractions. A verdant landscape and sleepy villages, beautiful castles and half-timbered cottages, some spectacular beaches and long stretches of coastline – it's not surprising that Hans Christian Andersen gained so much inspiration from the land of his birth.

Situated at the gateway to Scandinavia, Denmark shares many of the characteristics of its Nordic neighbours: liberal welfare benefits coupled with a high standard of living, and a style of government that aims at consensus and the avoidance of petty bureaucracy. Yet Denmark is also more 'European' and accessible than the rest of Scandinavia, and its appeal is universal.

The country consists of no fewer than 406 islands – at the last count – 97 of them inhabited. The only link with the Continent is the peninsula of Jylland (Jutland) that juts up rather like a finger from northern Germany and dominates the country, in area if not in population. With only five million inhabitants, Denmark is still by far the most densely populated Scandinavian country (though not the most populous); the figure of 291 people per square mile dwarfs neighbouring Sweden's 46.

Three ice ages have moulded the gently undulating landscape, which has since been transformed into a succession of neat model farms where every barn and farmhouse seems forever freshly painted. Grassland and wheat-fields sweep down to the roadside, while white medieval churches with distinctive step-gable towers rise above the village skylines. If you are anticipating any snowy peaks you'll be disappointed. The country's highest hill, Yding Skovhøj, 'soars' to a mere 197m (568ft).

Like their most famous of ancestors, the Vikings, today's Danes are an ebullient and outgoing people, though they are also the warmest and cosiest of

*D*anes can take pride in the past; but the flag still flies high over this seafaring nation.

tastiest pastries (*wienerbrød*) have to be seen to be believed. The profusion of delicatessen-type salads, cheeses and fresh fish is as tempting to the eye as to the palate.

As for shopping, porcelain, pewter and silver goods of the finest quality are manufactured here, and the Danish concept of functional yet aesthetically pleasing design is noticeable in most goods from household appliances to toys.

Centre of the country's government, administration and finance, the lively capital city of Copenhagen is home to nearly a third of Denmark's total population. It also boasts the oldest royal dynasty in Europe, now headed by Queen Margrethe II and her French-born husband, Prince Henrik.

Broad highways cut swathes through the city. Away from these routes, however, Copenhagen retains a well-preserved old-town area of winding cobbled streets, stuccoed houses and curio shops, as well as a network of canals. A fairyland quality pervades the city, with its 17th-century green copper

hosts. Entertaining friends in the home, surrounded by fine furniture and sitting down to a beautifully set table well-laden with choice food and drink, is one of the cherished ideals of Danish life.

Good food is something of a national obsession among the Danes. The amazing displays of open sandwiches (*smørre-brød*) and some of the world's roofs and domes, the legacy of Denmark's historical builder-king, Christian IV.

Crown jewel of this city of pleasure and imagination, the incomparable Tivoli lies right in the centre; more than a fun-fair, more than a park, it's a unique institution near to the hearts of all Copenhageners.

A strong sense of fantasy and colour fills the atmosphere in Copenhagen. Postmen wear bright red jackets and ride yellow bicycles. Chimney-sweeps pass by wearing black top-hats, using them to carry their lunchtime *smørrebrød*. Buses drive merrily along with red-and-white Danish flags fluttering each side of the cab.

Well before the phrase was sung by Danny Kaye, Copenhagen was known to be 'wonderful, wonderful' – a clean, green city full of gaiety, culture and charm, with a tradition of tolerance and humour. The chances are that if Hans Christian Andersen were able to return, he would still feel fully at home here today.

A Brief History

Well before the Vikings organized themselves into that extraordinary nation of seafarers, Denmark was inhabited by a people of hunters. Prehistoric relics of all kinds, some dating back to 50,000 BC, abound in Copenhagen's museums and the surrounding countryside, among them Stone Age flint arrow-heads and knives of expert craftsmanship. The oldest surviving costumes throughout the whole of Europe have been found in this area, as have various musical instruments, including over 30 examples of the famous Danish *lur*, whose hoarse notes seem strangely out of keeping with the long graceful S-shaped stem characteristic of the instrument.

Viking Age

The first written records of the Vikings appear around AD 800, at which time Viking raids on neighbouring European countries were becoming notorious. At their peak, these fearless warriors reached Newfoundland, were rounding the North Cape, and would make sallies to England, Holland, France, Spain, the Mediterranean, or even as far as the Caspian Sea. Prime examples of their boats are on display at the Roskilde Viking Ship Museum (see p.88), and an excavated settle-

Holger the Dane

The Viking Holger lived in the early 9th century. He travelled abroad and came back to Denmark in a time of trouble to help fight the country's enemies. Legend has it that he didn't die, but went to sleep, to wake whenever Denmark was threatened. As recently as World War II, a section of the Resistance adopted the name of Holger Danske. There is a famous statue of him in the Kronborg Castle at Helsingør (see p.84) – picture opposite.

ment at Trelleborg in West Zealand bears evidence of a camp capable of accommodating 1,300 warriors.

Danish raids upon England gathered in strength during the late 10th century and the first years of the 11th century, culminating in a full attempt at conquest. Canute (Knud) the Great, after meeting considerable resistance, finally became king of England in 1016. The union was to last until 1042.

Christianity had been introduced into Denmark in AD 826 by a Benedictine monk, and received the royal seal of approval in 961 when King Harald Bluetooth was converted by a monk named Poppo, who convinced him by seizing red-hot irons in his bare hands. A runic stone set up by Harald at Jelling in East Jutland records that he had 'won for himself all Denmark and Norway and made the Danes Christians'.

Medieval Times

In 1157, Valdemar I, styled the Great, came to the throne. He leaned heavily on the influ-

ence of Bishop Absalon of Roskilde, and this proved a partnership of critical importance to Copenhagen, then just a little fishing village called Havn. With its fine harbour on the Sound (*Øresund* in Danish) – that waterway between Denmark and Sweden which forms the main entrance to the Baltic – the village found itself well-placed on what was becoming one of the main trading routes of medieval Europe.

War-hero as well as statesman, Bishop Absalon fortified Havn by constructing a castle on its small harbour island of Slotsholmen in 1167; this is **9** now acknowledged to be the founding date of the modern city. The name Havn became Køpmannæhafn ('merchants' harbour') in 1170, and eventually København. Today, Slotsholmen lies at the heart of the city. The impressive Christiansborg parliament buildings now occupy the site, but you can see some remnants of Absalon's castle in their cellars (see p.51).

In the course of the reign of successive 12th-century kings, Denmark sorely over-extended itself in all directions, and for this it paid dearly in the 13th and 14th centuries. It had interfered in the government of Schleswig and Holstein (the dispute over these two border provinces lasted into the 20th century) as well as troubling the growing trade of the North German Hanseatic ports. So the Germans marched into Jutland. The Danish aristocracy seized the opportunity to curb the powers of its monarchy, and in 1282 King Erik V was forced to sign a Great Charter under which he would rule together with the nobles in the Council of the Danish Realm (*Danmarks Riges Råd*).

Nevertheless, Valdemar IV Atterdag (c.1320-75), probably the greatest of medieval Danish kings, led the country back on to a path of conquests and into new conflict with its Nordic neighbours – setting a pattern that was to last intermittently for centuries.

Denmark's hand was greatly strengthened when Valdemar's daughter, Margrete, married Håkon VI, King of Norway and Sweden. After his death, Margrete succeeded through the Treaty of Kalmar in 1397 in unifying the three Nordic powers under her nephew Erik VII of Pomerania. Indomitable Margrete ruled in his name, but was then struck down by the plague at the peak of her power in 1412.

During the later, true reign of Erik VII (1412-39), Copenhagen was enlarged. The city then became the official Danish capital under Christopher III of Bavaria in the 1440s; and when a university was founded by Christian I in 1479, it also became the country's cultural

HISTORICAL LANDMARKS

50,000 BC First evidence of human habitation in Denmark.

AD 800 The first written records of the Vikings emerge.

961 Christianity becomes the official Danish religion with the baptism of King Harald Bluetooth.

1016 Canute (Knud) the Great becomes King of England.

1167 Bishop Absalon fortifies Havn, thus laying the foundation for the modern city of Copenhagen.

1282 Erik V signs Great Charter, curbing the monarchy's power.

1340 Valdemar IV accedes to the throne and strengthens the country through a succession of conquests.

1397 The Treaty of Kalmar unifies the three Nordic powers – Denmark, Norway and Sweden – under Danish Queen Margrete's nephew, Erik VII of Pomerania.

1479 Christian I founds a university at Copenhagen, confirming the city as Denmark's cultural as well as official capital.

1596 Christian IV, the 'Great Builder', becomes king and presides over a period of great expansion.

1660 King Frederik III proclaims himself absolute monarch; Copenhagen is made a free city.

1728, 1795 Two massive fires devastate the city.

1801 Danish fleet destroyed in Copenhagen during an attack under the command of Admiral Nelson.

1901 Denmark's first real democratic government is elected.

1914-18 Denmark remains neutral during World War I.

1940 Denmark invaded by Hitler's forces, but a strong resistance movement grows, paving the way for rapid post-war reconstruction.

1949 Political neutrality is abandoned as Denmark joins NATO.

1972 Denmark becomes a member of the European Union (then the European Economic Community).

1992 In a referendum over 50 per cent of the Danes reject the Maastricht Treaty on European political and monetary union.

*E*lephants and castles feature on the central motif of this stained glass in Frederiksborg chapel.

passing through the 2½-mile channel between Helsingør on Zealand and Helsingborg in Sweden – the channel where ferries cross peacefully every few minutes these days. By then Denmark stood in a very strong position.

Forests had been cleared; new towns and villages had mushroomed everywhere. The scene was set for a period of 200 years marked by civil war against the nobles, the advent of the Lutheran movement in Denmark, and more wars to come with Sweden.

centre. By this time, the city's population had increased to about 10,000; Schleswig-Holstein was again under Danish rule; and a castle was being built at Helsingør (the Elsinore of Shakespeare's *Hamlet*) to enforce the payment of Sound tolls, for control of the Sound was vital to Denmark's strategic strength at the crossroads of the Northern Seas. Dues were exacted from each ship

The Reformation

In the 16th century, with the unprecedented spread of ideas, the latent, deep-seated discontent regarding abuses within the Catholic Church began to be brought out into the open. In Denmark, Catholic bishops had long been putting their wealth to political and military uses, and it was left to Christian III (reigned 1534-59) to break their stranglehold. He declared himself supreme authority of a State Church based on Lutheranism, which, since arriving from Germany, had made deep inroads. The bishops were imprisoned until they 'consented', their wealth commandeered to pay royal debts and train new pastors.

Meanwhile, the wars with Sweden lurched on disastrously, with fortunes turning in the favour of the Danes' enemies. By the latter half of the 17th century, Denmark had been forced to relinquish her remaining Swedish possessions and to cede also the east bank of the Sound to Sweden. This crucial waterway was now split down the middle, jointly controlled by the two Scandinavian powers, and remains so to this day.

As Denmark licked its many 17th-century war wounds, the city of Copenhagen held out two great consolations. It was made a free city in 1660 in acknowledgement of its bravery during a two-year blockade by Sweden. This meant that all residents were accorded the same privileges as the nobles. Secondly, under Christian IV it had experienced a wave of new culture and fine building. The 'Great Builder', as he was known, had effectively doubled the size of the city during the earlier part of the century, building the Christianshavn area just across the harbour channel on Amager Island as an Amsterdam-like complex of narrow canals, homes and warehouses, and going on to create a new housing district (Nyboder) to the north-west of Kongens Nytorv. His original yellow-wash rows of sailors' houses still remain standing today. On a grander architectural scale, he was responsible for the existence of so many of the monumental green copper roofs that make the Copenhagen skyline uniquely photogenic in the 20th century – most notably among them the Round Tower, the Stock Exchange and the magnificent Rosenborg Castle.

13

Absolute Power

As a result of the Swedish wars, Denmark was bankrupted and its country laid waste. Political and social upheaval were both inevitable.

In 1660, King Frederik III matched the mood of the moment and proclaimed himself absolute monarch, thereby depriving all the nobles of the Council of the Danish Realm of the powers they had enjoyed almost without a break since 1282. However, Frederik's absolute rule presided over a period of national unity, with a tightly controlled, well-organized central bureaucracy.

The early absolutist kings still waged several costly wars – mainly against the Swedish. Copenhagen suffered a terrible plague in 1711-12 which killed off 22,000 people – nearly a third of its inhabitants – as well as two devastating fires in 1728 and 1795 which necessitated major reconstruction of much of the city.

Despite these setbacks, the 18th century was highlighted by major social advancements.

Serfdom was abolished in 1788 (note the Freedom Pillar in Vesterbrogade, opposite the Central Station), and peasants threw off the yoke of the medieval landlord and worked for themselves. They moved away from the central farmhouse, to construct their own dwellings and smallholdings in the surrounding fields. This gave the Danish countryside its present character of a landscape dotted with farms, and was of enormous influence in the shaping of modern Denmark.

Napoleon and the 19th Century

Denmark found itself reluctantly involved in the European revolutionary wars of the late 18th century. By maintaining their participation with Russia, Sweden and Prussia in the League of Armed Neutrality – intended to thwart Great Britain's claim to the right of searching all vessels at sea – Denmark brought down upon itself the ire of the British. In 1801, a fleet under admirals Nelson and Parker sailed into

The combined Danish and French fleet arrives, greeted by a fanfare of gunpowder, in a 19th-century painting by Carl Neumann.

the bay of Copenhagen. During the ensuing battle, Nelson, so legend has it, raised a telescope to his blind eye so as to be able to deny having been aware of a signal to break off the engagement.

Afraid that Napoleon would take over the Dano-Norwegian fleet, Britain subsequently demanded its instant surrender. When the Danes refused to accede, Copenhagen was block-aded and in 1807 subjected to a three-day bombardment by the British Navy. Denmark had no choice but to hand over what was left of its fleet to the British, only to be forced immediately afterwards to agree to an alliance with Napoleon who was by then marching fast into Jutland.

When Napoleon was finally brought to his knees, Denmark emerged completely isolated **15** on account of this alliance. Norway, already the home to a vigorous separatist movement, was handed over to Sweden in 1814 in payment of war-debts, since Denmark's coffers had become empty. The formerly vast Danish territories overseas were reduced to Greenland, Iceland, the Faroes and the Virgin Islands.

Fifty years later Denmark was to lose also the duchies of

Schleswig and Holstein – a third of its home territory and two-fifths of its population – to Bismarck's Prussia. Following a spate of civil turmoil in Denmark provoked by the 1848 revolution in France, Frederik VII was forced to relinquish his absolute rule and hand over the reigns of power to the National Liberal Party.

A liberal constitution was drawn up with wide suffrage, and the Danish 'Golden Age' was all set to begin. Søren Kierkegaard shook up contemporary philosophy and Christian religion with radical new existentialist writings. Bertel Thorvaldsen, the great Danish sculptor, returned from Italy and left a profusion of monumental works in Copenhagen. Hans Christian Andersen was strolling the city streets, reading his fairy-tales to groups of admirers, and rapidly becoming world-famous.

Vestiges of power: a lovingly preserved cannon displayed in Copenhagen's Tivoli Gardens.

In the city, the old ramparts were demolished and new railroads, factories and workers' housing blocks sprang up, so that by the late 19th century Copenhagen was a thriving industrial centre. In the last quarter of the century, social insurance schemes began to make an appearance – a bold and pioneering development.

Meanwhile, changes were beginning to take place in the countryside. NFS Grundtvig, a leading European educationalist, had established his system of popular adult high schools in 1844 to improve the peasant's lot, and the first cooperative schemes were afoot.

The 20th Century

In 1901 an important landmark was reached in Danish constitutional history when a government based only on a majority in the lower chamber of parliament (*Folketing*) was appointed. The march of the common people brought them not only into the cities and urban areas, but also right into the political struggle. In 1915, the Liberal Democrats, Social Democrats and Radical Liberals jointly forced the abolition of electoral privileges in the upper chamber (*Landstinget*) and initiated a system of proportional representation for both chambers. At the same time, the vote was at last given to women and servants.

The new Danish society was put under severe strain in the process of adopting the compromises necessary to maintain neutrality during World War I. After the war North Schleswig voted itself back into Denmark, establishing the shape of today's border.

Industrial unrest, and the severe economic depression between the two world wars, failed to halt the progress of Denmark. In the sciences, theoretical physicist Niels Bohr of Copenhagen University was making fundamental contributions to atomic research. In architecture, Arne Jacobsen won a competition in 1929 for a circular, sun-rotating 'house of the future' capable of accommodating an aircraft on the roof. Elsewhere, in the design **17** of consumer goods – furniture, cutlery, glass, pewter, silver and textiles – Denmark set new standards, combining utility with beauty, to the point where 'Danish design' became synonymous with good, functional and aesthetic articles.

When World War II broke out in 1939, the Scandinavian countries issued declarations of neutrality, but on 9 April 1940 Denmark was invaded. Following a token struggle, the country's defences collapsed, and the nation fell under German control.

The Danish economy now found itself forced to adapt to the German market, and the country had no choice but to manifest a degree of compliance. However, the anti-Nazi sentiments of the vast majority of Danes were expressed by cold-shoulder treatment, and eventually acted upon through outright resistance. The Danes managed by various means to smuggle 7,000 of Denmark's 7,500 Jews out of the country to neighbouring Sweden.

The wartime king, Christian X, became the country's folk-hero as he rode out every day among the crowds. In 1943, the government resigned – it could no longer yield to German demands without losing the support of the population – and the running of the country was left to heads of departments. Nevertheless, the resistance was so organized and so dominant that Denmark was already a full member of the Allied forces by the time the war came to an end in 1945.

So began a new era of massive Danish reconstruction, finally resulting in the present modern-day society – one of the world's most successful attempts at a 'welfare state' – with a quality of life ranking certainly among the highest in the world.

Politically, Denmark abandoned neutrality when it became a member of NATO in 1949. Economically, it was a founder-member of the European Free Trade Association (EFTA), and transferred into the European Economic Community (subsequently the European Union) with the UK and Eire in 1972. It also played a part in the revival of Nordic unity after the war, joining the Nordic Council and the Nordic Council of Ministers.

Denmark today is one of the most prosperous countries in Europe, and its 5 million population enjoy an extremely high standard of living. Membership of the European exchange rate mechanism has ensured that its economy continues to grow in strength. The country made its biggest impact to date on the European Union in a 1992 referendum, when over 50 per cent of the population voted against the Maastricht Treaty (which lays the foundation for European economic and political union). The fact that Denmark's influence is felt so far beyond its frontiers testifies to its important role in the future of a cohesive and integrated Europe.

A chamber of the Danish parliament; members are elected by proportional representation.

What to See

You should have no problem finding your way around the delightfully compact and eminently walkable city of Copenhagen. Most of the important sights are contained within the central section bounded by the former medieval ramparts, and the city's many pedestrianized areas make exploring on foot a real pleasure. Copenhagen's abundance of leafy parks and gardens provide a welcome retreat from shopping or sightseeing, while its network of canals offers ample scope for waterside walks and gentle excursions afloat.

Rådhuspladsen

Every city has a heart somewhere, and Copenhagen's is without a doubt Rådhuspladsen (Town Hall Square). Most planned walks, like ours, begin from here, as do all the buses you will need for city tours and trips to surrounding countryside, castles and beaches.

Stand with your back to the red-brick Town Hall (*Rådhuset*) on the vast paved area of the Town Hall Square, and observe Danish life stroll or scurry by. Here also you'll find your first hot-dog stand (*pølsevogn*), where tasty Danish sausages are served in a variety of inexpensive forms. The unique Tivoli pleasure gardens (see p.42) are already visible over to your left, just beyond the eight-lane HC Andersens Boulevard, where you'll notice at once a very prominent feature of Danish life – the bicycle. At rush hours, there seem to be millions of them.

The capital's most famous pedestrians-only street starts just a few metres to your right. Strøget (pronounced *stroy*-et) winds its way along for 1km (here about ¾ mile) to another main square, Kongens Nytorv, changing name several times along the way and never officially called Strøget. Most of the surrounding area is pedestrians-only, too, and you can satisfy most of your shopping needs with hardly a motorized vehicle in sight.

COPENHAGEN HIGHLIGHTS

(See also Museum Highlights on p.53)

Amalienborg Palace: *Amalienborg Slotsplads.* Four elegant rococo palaces have been home to the Danish Royal Family since the 1750s; the changing of the guard at noon is a joy to behold. The palace is closed to the public, but a museum in King Christian VIII's Palace gives a glimpse of late 19th-century royal life. (See p.34)

Christiansborg Slot: *Christiansborg Slotsplads.* The castle constructed over Bishop Absalon's original 12th-century edifice houses a complex of museums as well as government ministries and the Danish Parliament (*Folketing*). *Royal Reception Chambers*: conducted tours June-August Tues-Sun 11am, 1pm and 3pm, September-May Tues-Sun 11am and 3pm; 27kr adults, 10kr children, free with Copenhagen Card. (See p.26)

Den Lille Havfrue: *Langelinie.* Edvard Eriksen's bronze sculpture of Andersen's forlorn Little Mermaid gazing wistfully out to sea is Copenhagen's most famous statue. (See p.36)

Rosenborg Slot: *Øster Voldgade 4A.* Christian IV's elegant Dutch Renaissance palace is a dazzling showcase for exhibits spanning 500 years of Danish royal history; highlights include the crown jewels and magnificent Long Hall. April-May and September-last week in October daily 11am-3pm, June-August daily 10am-4pm; 35kr adults, 5kr children, free with Copenhagen Card. (See p.45)

Rundetårn: *Købmagergade.* The astronomical observatory built by Christian IV in 1642 is one of Copenhagen's distinctive landmarks; access to the top of the tower is by a unique 209m (687ft) spiral causeway. *Tower*: September, April and May Mon-Sat 10am-5pm, Sunday noon-4pm June-August Mon-Sat 10am-8pm, Sunday noon-8pm. *Observatory*: October-March Tues-Wed 7-10pm; 12kr adults, 5kr children. (See p.43)

Tivoli: *Vesterbrogade 3.* Opened in 1843, this old-time pleasure park in the heart of the city still draws in the crowds. Daily end-April-mid-September; 38kr adults, 19kr children. (See p.42)

In the vast open square of Rådhuspladsen the statues leap to your attention – only a hint of the many hundreds scattered throughout the town. On the west corner of the square is the dramatic **Bull-and-Dragon Fountain** (1923), in copper, depicting a fierce, watery battle between the two beasts. Not far away sits a bronze version of Denmark's favourite son, storyteller Hans Christian Andersen, brooding by the boulevard that bears his name. For your third statue, glance left down Vesterbrogade. Dividing the highway near to the Central Station is the Freedom Pillar, erected between 1792 and 1797 to commemorate the end of serfdom for the Danish peasantry in 1788.

Next, to your right on Vester Voldgade is a statue that brings a smile to every Dane's face – the **Lur Blowers Statue**. Local legend has it that the two

*H*ans Christian Andersen, born in a slum, famed for his fairy **22** tales; a view over the city today.

ancient men on top will sound a note on their instruments if a virgin ever passes by – and though standing on the column since 1914 they've led a life of disconcerting silence!

The **Town Hall** was built between 1892 and 1905. Its main doorway is crowned by a statue of Bishop Absalon, the founder of the city (see p.9), in copper and 22-carat gilt. If you then direct your view to the roof above you'll see the rest of our introductory statues – six bronze figures of night-watchmen dating from various periods of the city's history.

Each section of the Town Hall bears a different style and imprint, but they come together architecturally in the same way as a patchwork quilt. The main hall and the banqueting room are impressive with their statuary and coats-of-arms – especially the view of the 44m (145ft) long hall from the first-floor colonnade.

There is only one way to see the Town Hall, and that is by guided tour. The two standard tours both leave from the entrance hall – each hour for the main tour and each half-hour for Jens Olsen's **World Clock**. Consult the lists there for the current schedules.

If it's a windy day, you'll be feeling a fresh breeze from the Baltic beyond the harbour. The Town Hall stands on the ancient shore-line and the waves would have been lapping at your feet in days gone by.

We have divided the sights into four convenient tours, designed for walking. Turn to the the map on the inside cover of this guide for easy reference.

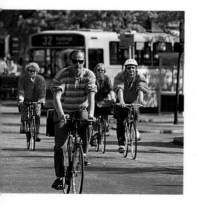

Walk 1

This first walk takes in some of the major sights, and the pedestrianized Strøget area.

THE OLD TOWN AND STRØGET

Crossing at the lights between Vester Voldgade and Rådhuspladsen, turn towards the Lur Blowers Statue and into the first narrow street on your left, Lavendelstræde. Here you will find typical Danish houses and shops from 1796, the year following the city's second great fire, as well as a view ahead of the massive masonry and archways of Copenhagen's fourth town hall. Built between 1805 and 1815, it now houses the country's principal law courts.

On the right as you turn into Hestemøllestræde is a corner house where Mozart's widow lived with her second husband, a Danish diplomat. Carry on across the next junction into Gåsegade, and look out for the gabled houses with 18th-century hoists at the top – furniture is traditionally hauled up by hoists, rather than being squeezed up narrow stairwells.

At the end of Gåsegade, on the left hand side, is a delightful little **square**, a suntrap on good days with a pretty fountain. The name of the square, Vandkunsten, means 'water artifice', and here Copenhagen's first water pipes were laid.

Cross into Magstræde and go back in time. At Nos 17 and 19 are two of the city's oldest houses, dating from 1640. Opposite is the excellent youth centre, **Huset** ('the house'). Besides having a jazz club and cinema, folk club, theatre and bars, Huset offers a wealth of advice, information and brochures for young travellers, including how to keep out of trouble – or deal with it if you're in it. The entrance is at Rådhusstræde 13.

Continue straight on, past interesting courtyards, Snaregade and finally some timber-framed houses, into **Gammel Strand** (meaning 'old shore'). As its name implies, this is the former edge of the city, and over the present-day canal you gat your first glimpse of mag-

*R*ush hour in the city centre, and still the Lur Blowers statue at Rådhuspladsen holds its peace.

nificent, green-roofed Christiansborg – now the home of parliament, but once a royal palace – built on an island.

Gammel Strand is a place to pause and prime your camera. It's a fine old waterfront. To the far right on Frederiksholms Kanal you'll be able to make out the arched entrance to the **25** colossal **Nationalmuseet** (see p.56). Immediately across the canal lies the untypical sight of a square-arched, yellow-ochre building with a decorated classical frieze, looking like a national tomb. That's really what it is – a monument to the great Danish sculptor, Bertel Thorvaldsen. Built between 1839 and 1848, **Thorvaldsens Museum** contains a mass of statuary, and the frieze depicts the sculptor's triumphant return from Rome in 1838.

Gammel Strand is one of the two principal starting points for canal boat tours, the other being in Nyhavn (see p.33).

A few yards further along, near Højbro Plads, stands the statue of the Fiskerkone (Fishwife), scarf on her head, wraps around her shoulders, wearing a stout apron and clasping a fish. Erected in 1940, she resembles the women who sit inside their stalls nearby every Tuesday to Friday morning, as they have for centuries.

In the near distance rears the magnificent equestrian **statue of Bishop Absalon**. Copper-green, displaying the warrior-

26

priest in chain-mail with axe in hand, the statue makes a most impressive picture against the background of red-tiled gable roofs and the soaring copper steeple of Skt Nikolaj Kirke (St Nicholas Church), now a café, restaurant and gallery.

As you cross over Højbro to Christiansborg Slotsplads, the square fronting on to the main entrance for the **Christiansborg complex**, look to your left over the bridge. The unusual sculpture you'll be able to see below the water is 'Mermaid with Seven Sons', attractively illuminated at night.

Christiansborg is the sixth castle or palace to have stood here since Absalon built his fortress in 1167 – pillage, fire and rebuilding frenzies having taken their toll. The third castle became the permanent seat of the king and government in 1417. The present edifice dates from the beginning of the 20th century, when an architectural competition for the design of a new Christiansborg was won by Thorvald Jørgensen. On 15 November 1907, King Frederik VIII laid the foundation-stone hewn out of the granite remains from Absalon's castle. Above this a vast plinth was made of about 7,500 boulders donated by 750 Danish boroughs, and then the palace was faced with granite slabs. Look up to see 57 granite masks of Denmark's greatest men. Covered in copper in 1937-39, the roof of Christiansborg makes an imposing addition to the city's typical green skyline.

The chapel, theatre museum, riding lodges and beautifully restored **marble bridge**, which managed to survive two disastrous fires in 1794 and 1884, help to give the palace a more venerable aspect than its mainly recent origins suggest.

The palace's interior holds enough delights to fill a whole day – see pp.51-2 for further details – but for the moment we'll continue along the canal

One sight not to be missed in Copenhagen is the exquisite marble bridge at Christiansborg.

as far as the highly ornamented **Børsen** (Stock Exchange), dating from the days of Christian IV. Its green copper roof is topped by a famous spire composed of four intricately twining dragons tails. Christian IV was influenced by the booming Netherlands architecture of his day, and in 1619 commissioned two Dutch brothers to put up this somewhat quaint building. The Stock Exchange has since emigrated to Strøget.

Glance to your left over the canal, past the Børsgade street flower market, and see another building rising straight out of the water, Venetian-style but with Dutch gable ends and a small copper tower in the middle. The building was originally a 16th-century anchor forge. However, in 1619 Christian IV transformed it into a sailors' church. **Holmens Kirke** (open Mon-Sat 9am-noon) is a real surprise when you walk inside: it's so small and cosy, giving an impression of warmth and wood. On the altar, the reredos and the pulpit, there's a veritable outburst of oak carving by Abel Schrøder the Younger, who became famous through these works alone.

Holmens Kirke remains a favourite with the Royal Family; in 1967 Queen Margrethe was married in the church to Prince Henrik, formerly the French Count de Laborde de

The humble pews of Holmens Kirke still serve as a comfortable refuge for seafarers of every kind.

Montpezat. It holds a special place in the affections of naval men also, an adjoining chapel (added in 1706-8) dedicated to sea heroes, from the 17th-century admiral Baron Niels Juel to Danish sailors who died in World War II. Two ship models hang from the ceiling of the church, a deep-seated tradition you'll note in many other Danish churches.

Up Admiralgade opposite the church, on the other side of the Holmens Kanal street, you approach the 70m (230ft) spire of Skt Nikolaj Kirke, which will have come into view regularly since the fishwives' corner. Destroyed several times by fire, it was rebuilt as recently as 1917. It is no longer used for services, only for public events such as art exhibitions.

Walk along Vingårdsstræde, and you'll find yourself in an area of jazz clubs, small bars and artists' dives; go over Bremerholm, on to Kongens Nytorv (see p.30), then left into the north-east end of **Strøget**.

Strøget is a charming and delightful traffic-free urban island to stroll along, by day or in the evening, with its numerous small bars, pavement cafés and excellent shops. It changes name four times during its ¾-mile course. At the Kongens Nytorv end, it begins as Østergade, then turns into Amagertorv, Vimmelskaftet, Nygade and Frederiksberggade.

Along the first stretch, off Østergade to the right, **Pistolstræde** is a picturesque alley lined with small restaurants and shops from five centuries of Copenhagen history. Return to Strøget and further on, at Amagertorv 6, you'll see a fine example of Dutch baroque, the Royal Copenhagen porcelain showroom. Shortly after is the 17-18th-century **Helligåndskirke** (Church of the Holy Ghost) with its grassy square.

Continue along Strøget. As you pass by Hyskenstræde and Badstuestræde, you're in an area of side-streets well worth investigating further if you're interested in antiques, curios and unusual little shops.

Strøget now opens out into a broad pedestrian area comprising the two squares of Gammeltorv and Nytorv and a **29** cluster of pavement cafés. On Nytorv, you have a full-frontal view of the simple yet powerful law courts. The **Caritas Fountain** on Gammeltorv is the city's oldest, dating from 1610. It is traditional (dating from the golden wedding of King Christian IX and Queen Louise in 1892) to make imitation golden apples dance on the jets on the monarch's birthday (now 16 April).

Strøget finally changes into Frederiksberggade, and 180m (200 yards) away lies our starting point, Rådhuspladsen.

Walk 2

KONGENS NYTORV AND THE HARBOUR

This walk begins at **Kongens Nytorv** (buses 1, 6, 28, 29 and 41 from Rådhuspladsen), the 'king's new square' of Christian V, dating from 1680 and still the city's largest square with 12 streets leading off it.

Setting the tone of the 3ha (8 acres) of Kongens Nytorv is **Det kongelige Teater** (Danish Royal Theatre), situated on the south-west side. This theatre is the country's most important cultural centre, the home of Danish national ballet, opera and drama. Originally opened in 1748, and rebuilt in 1874, it was briefly the stage of Hans Christian Andersen, who tried without success to become a ballet dancer there.

The house one door along, fronting the south side of Nyhavn canal, is said to be the most important work of pure baroque remaining today in Denmark. Called **Charlottenborg** because Queen Charlotte

Amalie lived here from 1700, it has functioned since 1753 as the seat of the Royal Danish Academy of Art.

Erected between 1672 and 1683 by the illegitimate son of King Frederik III, Ulrik Frederik Gyldenløve, Charlottenborg was of great architectural importance in Denmark. Not only were many country mansions modelled after this red-brick Dutch baroque design by a Dutch architect called Evert Janssen, but Ulrik also made the nobility build alongside him in Kongens Nytorv and develop the square in a manner worthy of its royal name.

Kongens Nytorv has space to relax and read. If writing postcards, look out for the red box.

Consequently, if you look around you'll notice a number of other fine buildings: **Thotts Palæ** (Thott's Mansion) in the north-east corner, built for the naval hero Admiral Niels Juel and now the French Embassy; and the quaint triangular building that stands between Store Strandstræde and Bredgade, the beautifully preserved 1782 **Kanneworffs Hus**. **31**

Centrepiece of the square is an elaborate equestrian statue of Christian V, with four classical figures seated submissively under his horse.

Now walk across the square towards **Nyhavn**. The name means literally 'new harbour', and you'll immediately notice the nautical flavour of this one-time 'sailors' street'. At this end of the canal, dug into the middle of the city in 1671 to enlarge the harbour facilities, stands a sizeable old anchor, a memorial to the Danish sailors killed in World War II.

Over the centuries the two sides of this canal have developed into a unique picture of old Copenhagen. Much painted and photographed, Nyhavn is today a mix of taverns and restaurants on its immediate north side, and elsewhere a collection of elegantly restored frontages, luxury apartments, some good restaurants and one superb hotel conversion of an 18th-century warehouse.

For two periods of his life Hans Christian Andersen lived in Nyhavn, first at No. 67 from 1854 to 1864 and later at No. 18. This is a street with everything – history, architecture, nightlife, a constant passage of colourful small boats and also a terminus for canal-boat tours as well as the hydrofoil service to Sweden.

Walk down Nyhavn (staying on the north side) until you come across a fine view looking out over the inner harbour to the Christianshavn area and the spiralling steeple of Vor Frelsers Kirke (see p.46).

With a waterfront like this, Copenhageners have every reason to smile.

A bespectacled Royal Life Guard takes his turn standing sentinel at Amalienborg Palace.

two wings. Four roads then converge at right-angles on the courtyard, while 16 bearskin-topped soldiers guard each of the palaces and corners, with an extra sentry posted at the gateway. The queen lives in the right-hand wing next to the colonnade, the queen mother lives in the adjacent wing, and the two princes live in the third, which houses in addition the Amalienborg Palace museum (see p.53). The fourth, directly to the left, is reserved as a guest house for state visitors.

Amalienborg was given its name after the wife of Frederik III, Queen Sophie Amalie, but the buildings burned down in 1689. The present mansions on the same site were originally designed as noblemen's homes by the court architect Nicolai Eigtved during a city expansion in the 1750s. After Christiansborg castle was de-

Bear round left to Skt Annæ Plads, a boulevard lined with consulates and fine old offices, then right into Amaliegade and through a wooden colonnaded archway into the stately square of **Amalienborg Palace**. All things here are in studied symmetry. On four of the eight sides stand identical mansion-like palaces. From each one jut stroyed by fire for a second time in 1794, the royal family slowly bought up Amalienborg from the nobles, and has lived there since. Today the palace is reckoned to be one of the finest rococo ensembles in Europe. Its centrepiece is a copper **equestrian monument** to King Frederik V.

The main Amalienborg attraction is the **changing of the guard**. At 11.30 each morning, when the queen is in residence, the guards leave their barracks near Rosenborg Castle and march through the city backstreets so as to arrive in the palace square just before noon, moving from one sentry-box to another in a series of foot-stamping ceremonies. Up to 70 guardsmen march in accompanied by a full band, black bearskins rippling in the breeze, wearing white striped blue trousers and highly polished boots, and, on festive occasions, red tunics with white shoulder straps.

The popular **Amaliehaven** gardens lie between Amalienborg Palace and the harbour. They were created by Belgian landscape architect Jean Delogne using French limestone and Danish granite, while the bronze pillars around the fountain were designed by Italian sculptor Arnaldo Pomodoro.

Keep strolling north along Amaliegade again to the junction with Esplanaden, where several sights come into view.

Frihedsmuseet (the Danish Resistance Movement Museum; see also p.54), located on one of the prettiest spots in

*T*he spectacular Gefion Fountain makes extraordinary use of both landscape and water.

town (especially at daffodil time) also offers the opportunity for a lunchtime snack at the cafeteria.

St Alban's Church resembles a typical English country church, and was indeed constructed by an English architect amid the green lawns of Churchill Park in 1887.

Andersen's Little Mermaid; entrance to Kastellet, beginning of the end of an afternoon stroll.

A spectacle that will arrest your attention even longer is the **Gefion Fountain**, Copenhagen's most spectacular, put up by the Carlsberg Foundation in 1908 and depicting the legend of the Nordic goddess Gefion, who turned her four sons into oxen and used them to plough the island of Zealand out of Sweden. Sculptor Anders Bundgaard's monument makes dramatic use of a small slope near the church, so that as the goddess and her 'sons' drive down it a massive spray of water flies up around.

Follow the right-hand path behind the fountain to Langelinie through delightful gardens, until you arrive at the most famous statue of all, the **Little Mermaid** (*Den Lille Havfrue*). In Andersen's fairytale, this tragic sea-girl exchanged her voice for human legs in order to gain the love of an earthly prince, but mutely had to watch as he jilted her for a real princess. In desperation, she threw herself into the sea and turned to foam.

To the dismay of both visitors and Danes, the mermaid

has frequently been vandalized. Once her head was sawn off; another time she lost her arm. Luckily, the workshop of sculptor Edvard Eriksen retains the original moulds from 1913, and new parts can be cast if necessary.

You can continue half a mile to **Langelinie** itself – a colourful quay when the tour ships are in – or take a detour into the Citadel gardens nearby.

Kastellet (the Citadel) was a cornerstone of Christian IV's defences of Copenhagen. The 300-year-old fort (most of it built between 1662 and 1725) is still in use by the army, and the church, prison and main guardhouse have resisted the assaults of time. It is a delightfully peaceful enclave, with a charming windmill (1847) and some remains of the old ramparts well worth seeing.

Within walking distance of the Citadel is **Nyboder** ('new dwellings'), erected between 1631 and 1641 by King Christian IV for his sailors. Yellow-painted, with steep gable roofs and shuttered windows, they form a well-preserved community of houses still inhabited by navy personnel, set in the triangle where Øster Voldgade meets Store Kongensgade.

Leave the Citadel garden by way of the southern exit onto Esplanaden, and turn towards **Bredgade**. The area between here and Kongens Nytorv is a residential quarter of substantial granite houses and quadrangles, once very fashionable, planned by architect Nicolai Eigtved at about the same time as Amalienborg. At No. 70 there is a plaque commemorating the death of philosopher Søren Kierkegaard in 1855. At No. 68 you'll find the **Kunstindustrimuseet** (Museum of Decorative Art), a fine rococo building and former 18th-century hospital (see p.54).

Almost next door, at No. 64, is Skt Ansgar Kirke, centre of the modest Roman Catholic community since 1842. A museum documents the history of Catholicism in the city since its virtual extinction in the Reformation of 1536.

Before two stately mansions on the corner of Fredericiagade appear the golden onion-shaped domes of **Alexander Newsky Kirke**, built for the

Russian Orthodox community between 1881 and 1883.

As Bredgade opens out at the junction with Frederiksgade, the great dome of **Marmorkirken** (Marble Church) rises high to your right. Measuring 31m (100ft) in diameter, this is one of the largest church domes in Europe. First planned around 1740 by Nicolai Eigtved as the centre-point of this new 'Frederik's Town' area (the church is also known as *Frederikskirken*), its foundation stone was laid by King Frederik V in 1749. However, by 1770 the Norwegian marble required for the building had become so expensive that the project was called to a halt, and it remained standing for a century as a picturesque ruin. It was eventually consecrated in 1894, Norwegian marble having been complemented by Danish marble from Faxe.

Inside, it's both impressive and beautiful. Carried on 12 stout pillars, the dome is decorated with rich frescoes in blue, gold and green. Outside, the church is surrounded by statues of personalities of the

Nyboder's rows of bright yellow-wash homes are still inhabited by Danish sailors today.

Danish Church, ranging from St Ansgar (who helped bring Christian religion to Denmark) to Grundtvig, the 19th-century educationalist. On the roof are 16 figures from religious history, from Moses to Luther.

This is an excellent place to rest before concluding your walk down elegant Bredgade. **39**

Walk 3

UNIVERSITY QUARTER AND PARKS

From Rådhuspladsen go west this time for a short way along Vester Voldgade and then turn right into narrow Studiestræde, the home to a motley collection of antique shops, bookstalls and boutiques gathered in an 18th-century setting.

At No. 6 Studiestræde a plaque records that HC Ørsted, discoverer of electro-magnetism in 1820, lived here. A few yards further on, at the corner of Nørregade, you will come across one of Copenhagen's oldest preserved buildings, the former **Bispegården** (Bishop's Residence), built in 1500 and now part of the University. Nearby on Bispetorvet stands a monument erected in 1943 commemorating the 400th anniversary of the introduction of the Reformation to Denmark. Over the square looms the sombre shape of the Cathedral (*Domkirken*) of Copenhagen, known as **Vor Frue Kirke** (Church of Our Lady). Bishop Absalon's successor, Sunesen, is said to have laid its foundations in the 12th century, but by 1316 it had already burned down four times. Later, two further constructions were destroyed – by the great 1728 fire

*T*he myriad light bulbs at the entrance to Tivoli are turned on in the afternoon, welcoming visitors.

and by British bombardment in 1807. The present church was reconstructed by VFK and CF Hansen in 1811-29.

Its large austere interior is relieved by a heroic collection of statues by Bertel Thorvaldsen; twelve massive marble Apostles line the aisle, while an orange-lit altar is surrounded with bronze candelabra and dominated by the famous **figure of Christ** by Thorvaldsen.

The main university block to the north of the Cathedral dates back in its present form only as far as the 1830s, but Copenhagen University itself was founded in 1479. This is a typical student area, with sidewalk cafés and a number of fascinating bookshops.

Behind the Cathedral and the University runs Fiolstræde, a delightful pedestrians-only street. Just down Krystalgade stands the Synagogue of Copenhagen, inaugurated in 1833.

Retrace your path down Fiolstræde, and make the detour into Skindergade, where you'll find **Gråbrødretorv** – a picturesque square surrounded by brightly painted 18th-century

Returning from lectures, a student pores over texts on display in a Danish bookshop.

houses which was the site of a Franciscan monastery until the Reformation. Cafés have proliferated here in recent years; it's a good place for a break.

Making your way in the direction of Købmagergade, first by Lille Kannikestæde, then going right along Store Kannikestræde, glance into the exquisite courtyard at No. 10 if **41**

Tivoli

Tivoli is magic, something you can't explain by statistics – an ambience created by chance and inspiration, you have to see and feel it to believe it. It's a reflection of the Danes' desire to enjoy themselves in pleasurable surroundings, a place for all the family and all generations to be together and have fun.

In the heart of the city and on the site of ancient fortifications, Tivoli is uniquely placed as a pleasure park. Here, you'll find two different worlds by day and by night. You can stay from 10am to midnight on one ticket (cheaper than cinema).

It's 400,000 flowers blooming at any one time, trees and pathways lit by 110,000 electric light bulbs (no neon here), free firework shows three nights a week, and a myriad of snack-bars, restaurants, cafés and beer houses serving anything from hotdogs to gourmet meals. (You can bring *smørre-brød* from the Vesterbrogade shops to a restaurant by the lake, buy yourself coffee and freely use plates, cutlery and napkins.)

It's a Chinese pagoda restaurant beside an arcade of lively slot machines; a concert hall offering everything from the Berlin Philharmonic to the Århus Fire Brigade Band; some 85 shops; merry-go-rounds for the kids; a pantomime theatre; coloured fountains by the lake; and a Tivoli Boy Guard's Band marching through like the Queen's Life Guard in miniature.

Five million people visit it each year, equivalent to the entire population of Denmark. Some 300 million have paid to gain admission since Georg Carstensen was granted a royal licence for the site in 1843. The 8ha (20 acre) pleasure park, the size of nine city blocks, is privately owned on lease from Copenhagen Council until 1995. Few fear for its continuance.

Open from the end of April to mid-September, Tivoli produces its own programme of events, available on the spot.

the gates are open. Admiral Ove Gjedde constructed this timbered mansion in 1637, dutifully echoing King Christian IV's wish that Copenhagen's beauty should be a joy forever.

The pleasant walking-street of **Købmagergade** is one of Copenhagen's oldest commercial thoroughfares. This is another street with Christian IV overtones, as here the ubiquitous builder laid the foundation stone of Trinitatis Kirke (Trinity Church) in 1637 and built the integral **Rundetårn** (Round Tower) in 1642 as an astronomical observatory. The Round Tower has been one of the city's most beloved landmarks for 300 years, even if it only reaches the modest height of 35m (115ft). It is more interesting to visit than the rather conventional church. You can walk to the top, but not by any ordinary means – steps would have proved impractical for

Outdoor performances at Tivoli are for the pleasure of all – even those on duty.

The wide causeway of the Round Tower spirals upwards at a very leisurely pace.

raising the heavy equipment needed there. Instead, a wide spiral-sloping causeway winds its way round for 209m (687ft) inside the tower. Not only did Czar Peter the Great ride up to the top on horseback in 1716 – his empress followed him in a coach-and-six.

Students have been living in the Regensen university hostel, opposite the Round Tower, since 1623. Most of the building standing today is 18th-century, with the notable addition of an arcade built in 1909.

One art attraction certainly worth a visit while in this area is the **Musikhistorisk Museum** (Musical History Museum) at Åbenrå 30, which holds a fine collection of old instruments and musical literature. Be sure not to forget **Davids Samling** (David Collection), which is located at Kronprinsessegade 30 (see p.54).

The street beside the Round Tower that is signposted Landemærket leads on to the main road, Gothersgade, and a wide expanse of parkland and some botanical gardens, as well as one of the most appealing castles to be found in any city.

Directly opposite the end of Landemærket is the **Kongens Have** park, laid out in 1606-7 when Christian IV announced that Christiansborg Palace was becoming too official and oppressive. At the same time, he began to build a small country mansion for himself in a corner of the site (it was then situated beyond the town walls) which he eventually expanded into **Rosenborg Slot** (Castle), since 1833 a royal museum of considerable grace and character (see p.58). Christian helped to plan this three-storey brick building in Dutch-Danish Renaissance style. It is as cosy a a castle as you'll ever find. It has all the frills and furbelows, turrets and towers, moats and battlemented gateways characteristic of a 'proper' castle, yet retains the atmosphere of a weekend retreat.

Gardeners will be interested in the **Botanisk Have** (Botanical Gardens) opposite Rosenborg, while art lovers should allow themselves time to explore the **Statens Museum for Kunst** (National Gallery) further north up Øster Voldgade. See pp.95 and 60 respectively.

From here, bus 10 will take you to Kongens Nytorv, while 75E (rush hours) will transport you back to Rådhuspladsen.

Walk 4

CHRISTIANSHAVN

Though there's so much to see within a small radius of Rådhuspladsen and Kongens Nytorv, it's worth spending a few hours just the other side of the harbour channel, crossing over the bridges Langebro or Knippelsbro into **Christianshavn**, and if time permits continuing on to the Amager villages of Store Magleby and Dragør.

The name Christianshavn, meaning Christian's Harbour, is derived from King Christian IV (once again), and the whole area looks very much like a slice of Amsterdam, reflecting his predilection for Netherlands architecture.

45

Take bus 2 or 8 from Rådhuspladsen to Christianshavn Torv then cross the main road and walk up **Overgaden oven Vandet** to see the Dutch-style warehouses, the narrow houses and small bars, all topped by hoists, and a scene of multi-coloured boats on the canal.

Turn the corner to the right into Skt Annæ Gade, and a Danish-Italian sight will meet you – **Vor Frelsers Kirke** (Our Saviour's Church). This brick and sandstone church was built between 1682 and 1696 under the direction of Lambert van Haven. The distinctive spire, with a staircase spiralling outside the structure, was added more than half a century later by Lauridz de Thurah, said to have been influenced at the time by the Sant'Ivo alla Sapienza church in Rome. A total of 400 steps (a third of them on the outside) lead from the entrance of the church to the gilt globe and Christ figure up on top of the spire, though you'll be allowed the rare experience of this outdoor climb – if you venture to take it – only in good weather.

Copenhageners like to pretend that de Thurah made a mistake by designing the spiral the wrong way round, and on realizing this suddenly threw himself from the top. The spire was completed, however, in 1752 and all the records state quite firmly that he lived on another seven years.

The inside of the church is unique, not simply because of the choir screen guarded by six wooden angels, nor because of the ornate white marble font, supported by four cherubs, nor even because of the 1732 altar, replete with allegorical statues and Dresden-like figures playing in the clouds. All this is crowned by the monumental organ, built in 1690 and several times remodelled, on the last occasion in 1965. Beautifully ornamented, the whole construction is supported by two large stucco elephants.

Elephants are something of a recurring theme in Denmark, perhaps traceable to the country's oldest order of chivalry, the Order of the Elephant. The central vault of the church is decorated with a monogram of

*H*eavenly steps wind their way up the length of the proud spire at Vor Frelsers Kirke.

Christian V, together with the royal coat-of-arms and a chain of the Order of the Elephant.

Our Saviour's is open Monday to Saturday from 9am to 3.30pm (10am to 1.30 pm in winter) and from noon to 1.30 pm on Sunday. You have to pay a small charge to climb the tower for the view of the city – though it may be undergoing repairs to keep it in condition .

Now retrace your path again along Skt Annæ Gade, and cross over the bridge towards the junction with **Strandgade**, opposite the Foreign Ministry. This area is a curious mixture of old and new. The Danish Centre for Architecture is a good example, a former warehouse at Gammel Dok. Turning left into the street of 17th- and 18th-century houses, take a peep into the cobbled courtyards, flanked by their numerous small living annexes. NFS

Grundtvig spent some years at No. 4B. At No. 6 in the early 18th century there lived Admiral Peter Wessel Tordenskjold – a Dano-Norwegian hero who won battles at sea but whose exuberant lifestyle ashore lost him many good neighbours. It's said that every time he called *skål* during his frequent banquets, a salute would be fired from two cannons at the main doorway, with many a sleepless night had by all until his death in a duel in 1720. **47**

Across Torvegade, blocking the end of Strandgade, lies the sombre **Christians Kirke**. It was built in 1755 by Nicolai Eigtved and possesses an unexpected interior layout, with arched galleries reminiscent of an old-time music-hall.

Next, the nearby Knippelsbro will bring you back towards the centre of the city, or there's an option to see some of Amager island and a quaint village by the sea.

Outlying Sights

Public transport takes you out to suburban Copenhagen. To go south to the municipalities of Amager island, catch a 31 bus at Christianshavns Torv, and after about 1½km (1 mile) change either to a 30 at Amager Boulevard or to a 33 at Sundholmsvej. You then drive through a large housing district and leave the airport route behind you (passing under the main runway) to reach the village of **Store Magleby**, untouched by time – except for the noise from the airport.

Here in an old farmhouse on the village street you'll find **Amagermuseet** (the Amager Museum), all laid out in old style, complete with furniture, bedrooms and kitchen. Begun in 1901, the collection was donated by villagers from the surrounding area. In a straightforward manner the museum explains the reasons for the Dutch atmosphere that prevails over this area.

The Dutch connection first began when King Christian II (reigned 1513-23) invited a colony of Netherlands farmers to come and improve soil cultivation in the area and provide the royal table with 'as many roots and onions as are needed'. He gave the Dutch special privileges to live in Store Magleby, which for centuries was referred to as Holländerbyen (Dutchmen's Town). They had their own judicial system and church (with services in Dutch or Low German only), and developed a bizarre local costume – derived from Dutch, Danish and French – a large collection of which is on display at the museum.

The Amager Museum stays open throughout the year Wednesday and Sunday 12-4pm, and May-September Thursday-Saturday 11am-3pm.

Hop aboard the 30 or 33 bus again for another 2½km (1½ miles) to the water's edge at **Dragør**, where the harbour is packed with small boats and the 18th-century village remains remarkably preserved. A maze of cobbled streets and alleyways leads off from the only traffic road. You can walk around between yellow-wash buildings and postage-stamp gardens building up a vivid impression of what life was like before the internal combustion engine.

Beside the harbour a 1682 fisherman's cottage (the oldest house in the town) has been imaginatively converted into the **Dragør Museum**, devoted to local seafaring history. The museum is open May-September Tuesday-Friday 2-5pm, Saturday and Sunday noon-6pm. From here, you can catch a 30 or 33 bus to make your way back to Rådhuspladsen.

Town Hall Square now provides the starting point for a trip to **Grundtvig's Memorial Church** in north-west Copenhagen at Bispebjerg. Here, a mere 10-minute journey from the centre (buses 16 and 19 from Rådhuspladsen), a total

E ven the weeds around the water pump lend themselves to the charming picture of Dragør.

of six million bricks have been laid as a monument honouring the man who was once called Denmark's greatest son.

Founder of the Danish residential high schools, Nikolai Frederik Severin Grundtvig (1783-1872) was a renowned educationalist, an austere parson and prolific hymn-writer. Grundtvigs Kirke, built in his memory, is also a monument to early 20th-century Danish architecture. The church's design, by Peder Jensen-Klint, is extraordinarily simple but effective. A few chosen masons, some of them employed from start to finish, carried through the project between 1921 and 1940. Everything is in pale-yellow brick – the 49m (160ft) tower and the vaults of the 22m (72ft) nave, all the stairs and pillars, the balustrades, altar and pulpit.

Stainless steel organ pipes (4,800 of them) look down on a vast, uncluttered nave. It's a fitting tribute to a man who composed 1,400 hymns, and a national monument that you should try not to miss.

Visiting hours are from mid-May to mid-September Monday-Saturday 9am-4.45pm or Sunday noon-4pm, and for the rest of the year 9am-4pm during the week and noon-1pm on Sunday and holidays.

A summer excursion by cycle and ferry — both common forms of transport in Denmark.

Museums

Hours may be subject to rapid change, and there's little consistency in admission charges. Some museums are free, many cost only a few kroner, while others charge a lot. Reductions for children are always available, varying between 50 and 80 per cent; sometimes they even get in free. A worthwhile investment is the Copenhagen Card (see p.137), valid for up to three days, which offers free entry to a large number of the major museums. To avoid disappointments, be sure to check up on opening hours and bus routes before setting out.

Christiansborg Slot (Christiansborg Castle)_

Today the castle houses government ministries, Parliament (*Folketing*) and also the Danish Supreme Court, as well as being the centre of a complex of museums, described below.

De Kongelige Repræsentationslokaler (Royal Reception Chambers). A fine starting point, but you must join a conducted tour. This is a no-touch museum with strict rules. One of the guide's first anecdotes is: 'Look at the roof here, held by epic pillars in the shape of male statues, heads bent to take the weight – a symbol of modern Danes paying their taxes …' In the entrance-hall, canvas slippers are provided for you to slip over your shoes, as you'll be gliding over priceless parquet floors.

Upstairs is a series of linked rooms with adornments ranging from imitation marble to the richly tapestried gold and green room where monarchs are proclaimed from the balcony overlooking the Castle Square (*Slotspladsen*) below. (Danish monarchs have not actually been crowned since the day of Christian VIII, though a crowd of 50,000 attended the proclamation of the present Queen Margrethe II in 1972.)

In the palace basement, the extensive well-preserved brick and stone **ruins** of the previous palaces are worth a visit.

Royal Reception Chambers: conducted tours June-August Tues-Sun 11am, 1 and 3pm; **51**

September and May Tues-Sun 11am, 3pm; Oct-April Tues, Thurs and Sun 11am and 3pm only. *Folketing*: tours every Sunday 10-11am and 1-4pm, also June-August daily except Saturday 10am-4pm. *Palace ruins*: Oct-April Tues-Fri and Sunday, May-September daily, 9.30am-3.30pm.

Teatermuseet (Theatre Museum)

Cross the royal riding grounds at the rear of Christiansborg – a scene dominated by a copper equestrian statue of Christian IX – and in an elegant terrace above the stables you'll discover an extraordinary theatre museums. The smell of horses seeps up through its 200-year-old creaky floorboards, and it has always been thus: at the Court Theatre's very first production in 1767, an authentic country odour was remarked.

The small auditorium and galleries are packed with Danish and international theatre relics – memorabilia of Ibsen, Anna Pavlova, Hans Christian Andersen, as well as playbills, costumes and photographs of Danish theatre history.

Open all year Wednesday 2-4pm and Sunday noon-4pm.

Tøjhusmuseet (Royal Arsenal Museum)

Tøj-husgade 3; buses 1, 2, 6 and 8 from Rådhuspladsen. Attendants wearing three-cornered hats and knee-length red jackets greet you in this vast building on the south-east side of Christiansborg. It's appropriate for a museum housing one of Europe's most important collections of military uniforms and historic equipment.

In this museum everything is laid out open-plan, with very little set behind glass. Cannon balls are piled high like potato stacks. Guns on display range from a 15th-century cannon of the time of Queen Margrete I to sophisticated new weapons. Three old military planes from 1909, 1921 and 1925 are suspended from the roof, while upstairs is a glittering display of uniforms and small arms. Open Tues-Sun 10am-4pm, closed Mondays.

MUSEUM HIGHLIGHTS

Amalienborg Palace Museum: *Christian VIII's Palace, Amalienborg.* See for yourself how the Danish Royal Family lived between 1863 and 1947. Open May-last week in October and 26-30 December daily 11am-4pm, at all other times Tuesday-Sunday 11am-4pm; 35kr adults, 5kr children, free with Copenhagen Card. (See p.34)

Den Hirschsprungske Samling: *Stockholmsgade 20.* A delightful museum set in parkland and devoted to 19th-century Danish art, notably Golden Age painters. Open Wednesday-Saturday 1-4pm, Sunday 11am-4pm, closed Monday and Tuesday; 20kr adults, children free. (See p.54)

Nationalmuseet: *Ny Vestergade 10.* The biggest museum in Scandinavia is a treasure trove of artefacts, from Stone Age rock carvings and Mongolian tents to Danish domestic interiors showing how people lived from the 17th century onwards. Open Tuesday-Sunday 10am-5pm; 30kr adults, children free, also free with Copenhagen Card. (See p.56)

Ny Carlsberg Glyptotek: *Dantes Plads 7.* The outstanding classical collection of Danish brewer Carl Jacobsen is brought together under one elaborate roof; exhibitions of Egyptian, Greek, Roman and Etruscan art feature alongside later works, including 73 bronze statuettes by Degas. Open May-August Tuesday-Sunday 10am-4pm, September-April Tuesday-Saturday noon-3pm, Sunday 10am-4pm; closed on Monday the whole year round; 15kr. (See p.58)

Thorvaldsens Museum: *Porthusgade 2.* The works of the prolific Danish sculptor Bertel Thorvaldsen are housed in the city's most distinctive building. Open Tuesday-Sunday 10am-5pm, guided tours in English Sunday 3pm; free. (See p.60)

53

Davids Samling (David's Art Collection)

Kronprinsessegade 30; buses 7 and 10 from Kongens Nytorv. European fine arts from the 17th and 18th centuries, a variety of Persian medieval art, ceramics and Danish 18th-century silverware. Open 1-4pm daily except Monday, all year.

Den Hirschsprungske Samling (Hirschsprung Collection)

Stockholmsgade 20. A charming little museum devoted to 19th-century Danish painting, sculpture and decorative art. Heinrich Hirschsprung, a rich tobacco merchant, donated the works to the Danish state at the turn of the century. Look out for the portraits and pristine landscapes of CW Eckersberg (1783-1853), a teacher at Copenhagen's Royal Academy whose meticulous style had a far-reaching influence. The romantic landscapes by Johan Lundbye date from the middle of the 19th century. A generation later, Peter Severin Krøyer worked to popularize social realist themes, while a unique Impressionist style was being developed by Laurits Tuxen as a student in Paris. Open Wed-Sat 1-4pm and Sundays 11am-4pm, closed Monday, Tuesday.

Frihedsmuseet (Museum of the Danish Resistance)

Churchillparken; buses 1 and 6 from Rådhuspladsen. A graphic record of wartime tragedy and eventual triumph. Every half hour, a loudspeaker commentary in Danish and English will guide you round the display. Open May-mid-September Tues-Sat 10am-4pm and Sunday until 5pm; mid-September-April Tues-Sat 11am-3pm and Sunday until 4pm.

Kunstindustrimuseet (Museum of Decorative Art)

Bredgade 68; buses 1 and 6 from Rådhuspladsen. A large display of European and Oriental handicrafts dating from the Middle Ages to the present housed in 1757 rococo buildings, a former hospital. There is a splendid garden as well. Open Tues-Sun 1-4pm.

Københavns Bymuseum (Copenhagen Museum)

Vesterbrogade 59; buses 6, 16 and 28 from Rådhuspladsen. Founded in 1901, this is a children's favourite with its scale model of the city centre (1525-50). Inside are clothing, sign-

boards, photographs, engravings and posters from the city's past. Here also lies the **Søren Kierkegaard Samling**, a collection of artefacts connected with the Danish philosopher. Open October-April Tues-Sun 1-4pm; May-September Tues-Sun 10am-4pm.

Marvelling at the ancient statues on display in Ny Carlsberg Glyptotek.

Legetøjsmuseet (Toy Museum)

Valkendorfsgade 13; buses 5, 14 and 16 from Rådhuspladsen. A fascinating collection of toys, from handmade to mechanical. Open all year 10am-4pm daily except Friday.

Louis Tussauds Voksmuseum (Wax Museum)

HC Andersens Boulevard 22. Wax models of famous Danish and foreign personalities, with light and sound effects. Open 27 April-18 September Mon-Sun 10am-11pm; rest of the year 10am-4.30pm daily.

Nationalmuseet (National Museum)

Ny Vestergade 10; buses 1, 2 and 6 from Rådhuspladsen. This is nothing less than a well organized labyrinth of artefacts ranging from Stone Age Danish rock carvings to Mongolian horseriding equipment and tents. It is the biggest museum in Scandinavia and consists of eight separate major collections, varying from prehistoric to modern Danish culture, Egyptian and classical antiquities, coins and medals, ethnographical and children's displays. Many have varying hours, so check before you plan your visits.

Visitors will be intrigued to study the prehistoric Denmark that led up to those extraordinary Viking times. Outstanding among Stone Age exhibits here is the Hindsgavle Dagger (1800-1500 BC), fashioned out of flint after bronze weapons in use elsewhere. Bronze technology came to Denmark after 1500 BC, and a wealth of interesting objects from the period are on view. The most striking exhibit is the Sun Chariot of 1200 BC. The Danes once worshipped the sun, imagining it just as it is here: a disc of gold riding in a chariot through the sky behind a celestial horse.

A vast repository of national culture, where every inch is of Danish design – Nationalmuseet.

Through its colonization of Greenland, Danish culture also opens doors on to Eskimo culture. The lively exhibition of huskies, igloos, reconstructed Eskimo camps and medieval clothes preserved in Greenland subsoil (ground floor rooms, Ny Vestergade entrance) is well worth a visit.

Open year round Tues-Sun 10am-5pm. Closed Mondays.

Ny Carlsberg Glyptotek

Dantes Plads 7, on HC Andersens Boulevard. A split personality museum with a touch of genius at either end of the psychic range. Basically, the Glyptotek was founded on the classical collection of Carl Jacobsen, a Danish brewer and art connoisseur (1842-1914) and was then developed by his family. Under its elaborate roof lies one of the world's foremost exhibitions of Egyptian, Greek, Roman and Etruscan art, with enough statues and artefacts to equip 100 ancient temples. As the museum was specially built around the classical collection, you'll find unique features like the breathtaking central hall, which appears to be transplanted direct from ancient Rome.

In complete contrast is the other collection: 25 Gauguins, three van Goghs, several Monets and seven Rodin statues all competing for attention in a compressed, four-room show, with a complete set of Degas bronzes – 73 delicate statues which won the painter posthumous acclaim as a sculptor.

Museum open May-August Tues-Sun 10am-4pm; September-April Tues-Sat noon-3pm and 10am-4pm Sunday; closed Monday all year round.

Rosenborg Slot (Rosenborg Castle)

Øster Vold-gade 4A; buses 14 and 16 from Rådhuspladsen, or S-train to Nørreport. The castle's 10,000 exhibits span Danish royal history over the past 500 years, though outside the dazzling cellar display of crown jewels the focus falls mainly on relics from founder Christian IV himself.

The castle's 24 rooms are arranged chronologically, beginning with his tower room study – still furnished in original style. The **Long Hall**, with its Swedish Wars tapestries, ornate ceiling and three almost life-size silver lions, is not to be hurried. In the hall is one of the world's largest collections of silver furniture, most of it from the 18th century.

The treasury, which is situated in the cellar, is home to the crown jewels. Besides the oldest existing specimen of the Order of the Elephant (see p.46) there are 18 cases full of crowns, gilded swords, pre-

Visit the Knights Hall at Rosenborg Slot and travel back through the silent years.

cious stones and coronation cups – even royal inkwells and tea-sets in pure gold. The centrepiece of this regal room is the 17th-century crown of the absolute monarchy – made out of gold, with diamonds, two sapphires and ruby spinels.

Open March-May and September-last week in October daily 11am-3pm; and June-August every day 10am-4pm.

59

Statens Museum for Kunst (The National Gallery)

Sølvgade 48-50; bus 10 from Kongens Nytorv and 75E (during rush hours) from Rådhuspladsen. Fine paintings from early Dutch to modern Danish in one light, airy building. The museum is particularly strong on 19th-century Danish landscapes, Matisse, representative Dutch and Flemish works of art from Rembrandt to Paulus Potter, an Italian collection including Titian and Tintoretto; and perhaps the world's finest collection of Dürer prints. The bold colours employed by the Danish painter Niels Larsen Stevns (1864-1941), one of the great painters of his day, catch the eye. Open all year Tues-Sun 10am-4.30pm, until 9pm Wednesday; closed Monday.

Thorvaldsens Museum

Porthusgade 2; buses 1, 2 and 6 from Rådhuspladsen. This is another museum of classical intent. Roman and Greek gods and goddesses gazing down at you, however, are all 19th-century revivals of antiquity – the work of Bertel Thorvaldsen (1770-1844), the greatest of Danish sculptors and Copenhagen's only honorary citizen.

Returning after 40 years in Rome – the Danish government fetched him back in triumph – he devoted his library, collection and fortune to the creation of a museum of his own works, choosing a young architect, Gottlieb Bindesbøll, to design it. The result was one of Copenhagen's most distinctive, untypical buildings, with a decorated ochre façade, and interior walls and ceilings in black, reds, blues and oranges that throw into high contrast the pure white plaster and marble of Thorvaldsen's sculpture.

The ground-floor display in 21 interlinked sections shows why he has been called one of the greatest sculptors since the days of the Caesars – a noble array of chaste classic gods, popes and aristocracy, an idealized vision of mankind with never a wart in sight. Open all year round Tues-Sun 10am-5pm; tours 3pm on Sunday.

Excursions

In a country of 44,030sq km (17,000 sq miles), nature has ingeniously divided Denmark into more than 400 islands so that you are never more than 50km (30 miles) from the sea. Copenhageners have their own beach, woodlands and a wide lake area, and within the city boundary you can easily organize an excursion including a boat trip, windmills and water-mills, a royal country castle and genuine village settings.

OPEN-AIR FOLK MUSEUM AND LYNGBY LAKE

Initially we're aiming for **Frilandsmuseet** (Open-Air Folk Museum) at Sorgenfri, 13km (8 miles) north of the city, accessible by car along the A3 and A5 main roads, by direct bus 184 from Nørreport terminus in town, or by S-train, line Cc to Sorgenfri station. Another more interesting and adventurous route is to take the same train and change at Jægersborg station to the little red one-coach train known as *Grisen* ('The Pig'), which will drop you at Fuglevad Station near the museum's back entrance.

Forty farmhouses, cottages, workshops, and a Dutch-type windmill are sprinkled about the 36ha (90acre) site of Frilandsmuseet – all furnished in authentic style with everything down to combs and portraits.

A table for four stands as testimony to a long, deep-seated tradition of Danish hospitality.

Broadly, the buildings are split into geographical groups laid out along country lanes together with bridges and village pumps, all authentically landscaped. Each of these has been transplanted, tile by tile, timber by timber, from its original location. You'll find a Zealand group, a Jutland and a Faroes group, etc. Homes of all classes are represented – from peasant to landowner, as well as artisan and farmer.

The smell of old timber and tar pervades the rooms. Geese and sheep are driven along the lanes. Displays of folk danc-ing, sheep shearing, threshing and weaving are given during the summer. There are horse-and-carriage rides, and picnic spots in tree-lined meadows.

Both the opening hours and times of guided tours (in English) tend to change from one year to the next, so before you set out for Frilandsmuseet, be sure to refer to the daily press or the Copenhagen tourist information office (see p.134).

Allow yourself time when the weather is fine to stroll half a mile down the main road towards Lyngby and a rural boat ride scarcely equalled in any capital city. On your left is the whitewalled, baroque castle, **Sorgenfri Slot** (closed to the public), built in the 18th century by the man who also designed the spire of Vor Frelsers Kirke (see p.46). Proceed over Mølleåaen (the Mill Stream).

Gentle breezes waft the summer air across rolling stretches of Danish countryside.

Follow signs to the right for *Lyngby Sø – Bådfarten* ('Lyngby Lake – Boat Trip') to find at the quayside two venerable canopied boats that have plied the four lakes since the 1890s. **63**

A 45-minute **cruise**, either Lyngby-Frederiksdal or Lyngby-Sophienholm, gives you a flavour of these delightful tree-covered backwaters and broad reedy lakes. The boats operate from May to September or October, depending on weather.

As you float by, you'll pass the 1803 mansion of Marienborg amidst the trees, the offi-cial summer residence of Danish prime ministers; further on is Frederiksdal with its **castle** on a hill above. This former royal house has been lived in by the same family since 1740.

An alternative trip will take you to **Sophienholm Mansion** (1805), now a community cultural arts centre. Outdoor café tables give an idyllic view over the waters of Bagsværd Sø.

Back on Lyngby quay, the 184 bus can take you direct to town again, or it's a short walk to Lyngby S-train station to re-join the A- or Cc-line service.

*B*oating on the lakes is just one of the many pleasant ways to spend a day in the countryside.

Hotels and Restaurants in Copenhagen

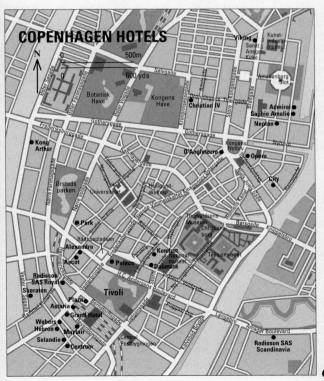

Recommended Hotels

Copenhagen's hotels tend to be clustered around the centre. All are within a very short walking distance of the city's main sights – Rådhuspladsen, the lively shopping street Strøget and the Tivoli Gardens. The main railway station is a mere 5 minutes walk away from the centre, while the airport lies a brief 20-minute journey away by car or bus.

We have listed the following Copenhagen establishments according to their different price categories: expensive (above 1,200kr), moderate (600-1,200kr) and inexpensive (below 600kr). Prices are based on the cost per night of a double room with en suite bath or shower (unless indicated otherwise), including service charge, VAT and breakfast.

It is always advisable to reserve ahead of your stay. The city is at its busiest in the summer months (June to August), but conferences ensure that hotels are kept busy throughout the year.

We have included hotels within easy reach of the city, as well as some in more distant places that are suitable for excursions. Should you come across an establishment worth recommending, we would be pleased to hear from you.

EXPENSIVE

Hotel d'Angleterre
Kongens Nytorv 34
1050 Copenhagen K
Tel. 33 12 00 95
Fax 33 12 11 18
One of the oldest deluxe hotels in the world, Hotel d'Angleterre was originally built in 1630, and reconstructed in 1755. This is one of those classic establishments where bathrooms are adorned with marble, gold-plated fittings and snow-white towels. Inside there are two restaurants: Le Restaurant d'Angleterre, serving a menu of international food that is changed every few days; and Restaurant Wünblad, which offers more traditional Danish fare. A great favourite with business people, and much appreciated by the tourists as well. 130 rooms, including 18 suites.

Neptun

Skt. Annæ Plads 14-20
1250 Copenhagen K
Tel. 33 13 89 00
Fax. 33 14 12 50

Originally built in 1854, the hotel is decorated with beautiful Scandinavian antiques and contemporary paintings. Gourmet restaurant in cosy surroundings, and an attractive courtyard. 136 rooms.

71 Nyhavn Hotel

Nyhavn 71
1051 Copenhagen K
Tel. 33 11 85 85
Fax 33 93 15 85

A former warehouse in a glorious setting on Copenhagen's waterfront, 71 Nyhavn Hotel is full of character. The rooms are small but many retain their wooden beams. (Ask for a room with a view.) The restaurant Pakhuskælderen serves fine Danish cuisine, while Fyrskibet (an old restored Danish lightship anchored outside the hotel) is available for private functions. 82 rooms, including 6 suites.

Palace

Rådhuspladsen 57
1550 Copenhagen V
Tel. 33 14 40 50
Fax 33 14 52 79

An imposing historical landmark located on the Town Hall Square,

the Palace has been carefully renovated and modernized over the years so as to offer a high standard of accommodation, with spacious bedrooms and health club facilities. The hotel's one restaurant, Brasserie on the Square, serves a good selection of both international and Danish cuisines, while elsewhere there is a cocktail bar. 155 rooms, including 4 suites.

The Plaza

Bernstorffsgade 4
1577 Copenhagen V
Tel. 33 14 92 62
Fax 33 93 93 62

A comfortable and well equipped hotel, with beautifully appointed rooms and a very high standard of decoration throughout. The attractive Library Bar, brimming with antique books and works of art, is a fine place to enjoy a drink, as well as being one of the most civilized *rendez-vous* in Copenhagen. The Flora Danica restaurant offers Danish-style buffets. 93 rooms.

SAS Royal

Hammerichsgade 1
1611 Copenhagen V
Tel. 33 14 14 12
Fax 33 14 14 21

Dating only from 1960, this modern hotel follows the best tradition of avant-garde Danish design. The **67**

Summit restaurant, situated on the 20th floor, offers a spectacular panoramic view of the city. Down in the lobby, the more informal Café Royal serves sandwiches and snacks. A haven for business people, it also attracts tourists during holidays, especially from June to August. Sauna. 265 rooms.

SAS Scandinavia

Amager Boulevard 70
2300 Copenhagen S
Tel. 33 11 23 24
Fax 31 57 01 93
Another well equipped hotel, with all the facilities and comfort you would expect of this internationally established chain. Indoor swimming pool, sauna. Largest hotel in the capital, with 542 rooms.

Sheraton

Vester Søgade 6, PO Box 337
1601 Copenhagen V
Tel. 33 14 35 35
Fax 33 32 12 23
Modern, 17-storey building, offering a whole range of facilities, including a health club and on-site parking. The Blue Garden restaurant serves both international and Danish cuisine, while the Café R offers light meals and snacks. In addition there are two bars: the Red Lion English pub and Amphora Bar. 435 rooms, 36 suites.

MODERATE

Admiral Hotel

Tolbodgade 24-28
1253 Copenhagen K
Tel. 33 11 82 82
Fax. 33 32 55 42
Standing beside the harbour, the hotel was formerly a granary, built 200 years ago. Comfortably converted, it has retained the wooden beams in the rooms. With its own restaurant, and sauna. 366 rooms.

Alexandra

HC Andersens Boulevard 8
1553 Copenhagen V
Tel. 33 14 22 00
Fax 33 14 02 84
A lovely old hotel, pleasantly decorated, with light, airy rooms and excellent facilities (including underground parking). Although the hotel has no restaurant, the bar serves breakfast. 63 rooms.

Ascot

Studiestræde 61
1554 Copenhagen V
Tel. 33 12 60 00
Fax 33 14 60 40
Set in a distinguished old building, a few steps from City Hall, this hotel is pleasantly decorated with a mixture of antiques and modern furniture. There is no restaurant, but breakfast buffet and room ser-

vice are both available. 140 rooms and suites, wih a range of studios and penthouse apartments.

Grand Hotel

Vesterbrogade 9A
1620 Copenhagen V
Tel. 31 31 36 00
Fax 31 31 33 50

This historical building has been carefully modernized in a manner that preserves much of its original character. Lovely rooms, tastefully decorated. Restaurant Oliver and Grand Bar. 146 rooms, 2 suites.

Komfort

Løngangsstræde 27
1468 Copenhagen V
Tel. 33 12 65 70
Fax 33 15 28 99

A welcoming modern hotel, with bright rooms, a lively English pub, and restaurant. Also underground parking. 202 rooms, including two quads and 7 triples.

Mayfair

Helgolandsgade 3
1653 Copenhagen V
Tel. 31 31 48 01
Fax 31 23 96 86

A turn-of-the-century hotel which has been recently refurbished, the Mayfair is privately owned, and offers a cosy atmosphere coupled with a very high standard of per-

sonal service. Its restaurant serves a large buffet-style breakfast. 101 rooms, including 4 suites.

Opera

Todenskjoldsgade 15
1055 Copenhagen K
Tel. 33 12 15 19
Fax 33 32 12 82

A few steps away from the Royal Theatre, the building dates from 1869 and has recently undergone renovation, with 'Olde England' décor now installed throughout. An excellent choice for families. 87 rooms.

Hotel Triton

Helgolandsgade 7-11
1653 Copenhagen V
Tel. 31 31 32 66
Fax. 31 31 69 70

A comfortable hotel located to the west of the centre. There is a bar, though no restaurant. 123 rooms.

Webers

Vesterbrogade 11B
1620 Copenhagen V
Tel. 31 31 14 32
Fax 31 31 14 41

A modern building fitted out with reproduction antique furniture and also offering a lovely courtyard. The restaurant serves breakfast only, but there is also a bar. Health club facilities. 103 rooms.

69

INEXPENSIVE

Astoria

Banegårdspladsen 4
1570 Copenhagen V
Tel. 33 14 14 19
Fax 33 14 08 02

The Astoria dates from 1936, and is an excellent architectural example of cubist style. It has been lovingly preserved, though the rooms have been updated to meet modern tastes. It is particularly suitable for families, and the recent introduction of bunk beds has proved a great success with both families and backpackers. The hotel serves a good breakfast buffet. It is recommended that guests book in advance. 94 rooms.

Centrum

Helgolandsgade 14
1653 Copenhagen V
Tel. 31 31 31 11
Fax 31 23 32 51

An economy/tourist class hotel located in a quiet part of the city to the west of the centre. The building dates from the Victorian era, but the hotel has been fully modernized. Half the rooms have a private bathroom and colour TV. The budget rooms are without private facilities but guests will find modern bathrooms available on every floor. There is a bar and a restaurant that serves breakfast only (it is available, however, for groups if lunch and/or dinner has been ordered together with accommodation). 80 rooms.

Christian IV

Dronningens Tværgade 45
1302 Copenhagen K
Tel. 33 32 10 44
Fax 33 32 07 06

Located almost on the doorstep of the lovely King's Garden, this is a small airy hotel which is efficiently run. Rooms tend to be neat and bright, and are fitted out with modern Danish furniture. There is no restaurant on site, but breakfast is served in a pleasant dining room. 42 rooms.

City

Peder Skramsgade 24
1054 Copenhagen K
Tel. 33 13 06 66
Fax 33 13 06 67

Set in an elegant town house, the City has a definite international feel to it, clearly expressed in the hotel's brand new, striking modern décor. Personal service, however, remains high on the management's list of priorities, making for a hospitable, friendly atmosphere. Although the restaurant only serves breakfast, there is also a café on site. 85 rooms.

Cosmopole

Colbjørnsensgade 5-11
1652 Copenhagen V
Tel. 31 21 33 33
Fax 31 31 33 99

A superior tourist-class hotel, furnished in a modern Scandinavian style, with simple, unpretentious décor and service. 208 rooms.

Danmark

Vester Voldgade 89
1557 Copenhagen V
Tel. 33 11 48 06
Fax 33 14 36 30

A family-run hotel that is conveniently situated right in the heart of Copenhagen close to Strøget and Rådhuspladsen, in a modern, bright building. Rooms are tastefully furnished in subdued Scandinavian style, all with bathrooms and television. Only breakfast is served, though drinks are available throughout the day. Also underground parking and conference facilities. 51 rooms.

Excelsior

Colbjørnsensgade 4
1652 Copenhagen V
Tel. 31 24 50 85
Fax 31 24 50 87

Located just west of the city centre, the hotel offers rooms with telephone, television and mini-bar. 95 rooms and 1 apartment.

Hotel Hebron

Helgolandsgade 4
1653 Copenhagen V
Tel. 31 31 69 06
Fax 31 31 90 67

Quiet location close to the heart of the city, with its rooms benefiting from the soundproof double glazing installed throughout the hotel. Rooms are bright, spacious and well equipped. Suitable for families. The hotel's restaurant serves breakfast only. 112 rooms.

Kong Arthur

Nørre Søgade 11
1370 Copenhagen V
Tel. 33 11 12 12
Fax 33 32 61 30

Inaugurated in 1882, this charming hotel has retained much of its original charm.It is situated beside the Peblinge Lake. A family-run establishment, Kong Arthur is a popular choice with both Danish and foreign visitors, who appreciate the friendly and thoroughly Danish atmosphere. The pleasant breakfast room overlooks a pretty patio, and there is a choice of restaurants, with the Brøchner offering Danish and French dishes, and the Stick'n'Sushi specializing in Japanese dishes. Good value for money. There are also sauna facilities and 40 free parking lots. 107 rooms, 7 suites.

Selandia

Helgolandsgade 12
1653 Copenhagen V
Tel. and fax 31 31 46 10
An unpretentious, functional hotel with comfortable rooms, most of which have private bath or shower, and friendly service. The hotel's restaurant serves breakfast only, but drinks are available throughout the day. 84 rooms.

Sophie Amalie Hotel

Sankt Annæ Plads 21
1250 Copenhagen K
Tel. 33 13 34 00
Fax 33 11 77 07
Situated on the harbour-front and adjacent to Amalienborg Palace, this hotel was recently refurbished to provide good accommodation at a reasonable price. Lovely views of the new Copenhagen harbour promenade and the picturesque buildings surrounding Nyhavn and Amalienborg. 134 rooms.

Hotel Viking

Bredgade 65
1260 Copenhagen K
Tel. 33 12 45 50
Fax. 33 12 46 18
Located along the once fashionable stretch of Bredgade, this hotel has the atmosphere of an English bed and breakfast. Restaurant and bar. 90 rooms.

FURTHER AFIELD

Eremitage

Lyngby Storcenter 62
2800 Lyngby
Tel. 42 88 77 00
Fax 42 88 17 82
A modern hotel, 10km (6 miles) from central Copenhagen, and five minutes' walk from Lyngby Station. Recent décor, with the emphasis placed on Scandinavian furnishings. Contemporary Danish art brightens up the walls. Comfortable rooms with all facilities. Euro Brasserie Restaurant; Euro Bar and Euro Café. Conference facilities. Golf club, lakes, shops, museums and other attractions all within easy reach. Private parking. 117 rooms and suites. A few 1- and 2-bedroom apartments.

Hellerup Parkhotel

Strandvejen 203
2900 Hellerup
Tel. 31 62 40 44
Fax 31 62 56 57
Set in the executive neighbourhood 5km (3 miles) to the north of central Copenhagen, this is a first-class hotel with every facility, including a health club. Recently refurbished in modern style, the hotel offers a choice of two restaurants, one serving gourmet food, the other Italian. 71 rooms.

Hotel Hillerød

Milnersvej 41
3400 Hillerød
Tel. 48 24 08 00
Fax 48 24 08 74

In the delightful town of Hillerød, the hotel is a mere 40-minute train journey from central Copenhagen. Conveniently situated for exploring the excellent sandy beaches of North Zealand, or for trips further afield over to Jutland and Sweden. Modern rooms, each with private terrace, bathroom, WC and kitchenette. 61 rooms in all.

Marienlyst

Nordre Strandvej 2
3000 Helsingor
Tel. and fax. 49 20 33 90

Well placed for anyone wishing to visit Kronborg. Most rooms have views looking out over the beach and sea. The hotel also has a large restaurant, sauna and swimming pool. 78 apartments.

Marina

Vedbæk Strandvej 391
2950 Vedbæk
Tel. 42 89 17 11
Fax 42 89 17 22

Situated midway between Copenhagen and Helsingør, the hotel has stunning views over the harbour and across the Øresund strait to Sweden. All modern facilities are provided for the comfort of guests, including a restaurant (with live music and dancing in the evening), supermarket, sauna, wooded paths for walking and jogging, conference rooms, garage, mini-bar and television. There are 127 rooms and 13 apartments.

Hotel Prindsen

Algade 13
4000 Roskilde
Tel. 42 35 80 10
Fax 42 35 81 10

A thoroughly refurbished hotel in the centre of Denmark's oldest royal city, situated about 5 minutes from the Cathedral. Friendly atmosphere and efficient service. Restaurant and bar as well as private parking. Children under 12 can stay without charge in their parents' rooms. 40 rooms in all.

Hotel Skandia

Bramstræde 3
3000 Helsingør
Tel. 49 21 09 02
Fax 49 26 54 90

An old family-run hotel, just 2 minutes' walk from the railway station. No television or radio in the rooms – helping to retain the authentic atmosphere and rustic charm of this small establishment. All the bedrooms are individually decorated. 43 rooms.

Recommended Restaurants

With over 2,000 restaurants, many of them serving ethnic cuisine, Copenhagen is something of a gourmet's paradise. Whether you fancy a quick coffee and *wienerbrød* or a five-course feast, you'll have plenty of places to choose from. There are 28 eating establishments alone inside the Tivoli Gardens, while the nearby Scala Centre has numerous bars and restaurants of all types. For lunch, cafés offer the best option for economy-minded diners, with a selection of hot dishes and filling *smørrebrød* at reasonable prices. Dinner can be as light or as heavy as you like, and many places offer traditional Scandinavian open table, where you eat as much as you can for a set charge. All cafés and restaurants have a menu displayed outside, so you can check prices before entering.

The establishments detailed below offer a cross-section of what is available. We have arranged them according to three price categories: expensive (above 300kr), moderate (150-300kr) and inexpensive (below 150kr). Prices are based on the cost of a meal per person, including tax but excluding drinks. Remember that the high import duty on wine can add considerably to the final bill. For an up-to-date listing of all kinds of eating establishments, consult the free monthly magazine, *Copenhagen This Week* (see p.129).

EXPENSIVE

Bourgogne
Dronningens Tværgade 2
1302 Copenhagen K
Tel. 33 12 03 17
In a romantic cellar beneath 300 year-old Moltke Palace. French and Danish cuisine. Open Monday to Saturday from 5pm to 10pm.

Cassiopeia
Gammel Kongevej 10
1610 Copenhagen
Tel. 33 15 09 33
A charming lakeside establishment located in the same complex as the planetarium. The restaurant serves a selection of typical Danish cuisine. Open every day from 11.30am until 11pm.

Divan 1

Vesterbrogade 3
1620 Copenhagen V
Tel. 33 11 42 42
One of a wide array of restaurants to be found at Tivoli Gardens, in this case serving mainly international cuisine. Open from end of April to mid-September every day noon until midnight .

Divan 2

Vesterbrogade 3
1620 Copenhagen V
Tel. 33 12 51 51
Also set in Tivoli Gardens, offering gourmet outdoor dining. Open daily 11.30am until midnight from end April to mid-September.

Els

Store Strandstræde 3
1255 Copenhagen K
Tel. 33 14 13 41
The elegant 19th-century decor of this delightful restaurant close to Kongens Nytorv complements the stylish cuisine. Fish is a speciality, and the menu changes every day. Reservations are strongly advised.

Les Etoiles

Dronningens Tværgade 43
1302 Copenhagen K
Tel. 33 15 05 54
A restaurant allowing a civilized space between tables, and serving classic French cuisine. Open Tuesday to Friday noon to 3pm, 6pm to 10pm, and Saturday 3pm to 10pm; closed Sunday and Monday.

Færgen Sjælland

Christians Brygge Kajplads 114
1559 Copenhagen
Tel. 33 13 43 30
Set on an old ferry moored in the river about half a mile from Rådhuspladsen, this acclaimed restaurant has a number of dining rooms with a range of menus offering mainly international cuisine. Extensive wine list and live entertainment. Open Monday to Thursday noon to midnight, Friday until 1am, Saturday 6pm to 1am.

Den Gule Cottage

Strandvejen 506
2930 Klampenborg
Tel. 31 64 06 91
French-Danish cuisine served in the attractive setting of a cottage with views on to the sea. Reservations are essential. Open every day from noon to 3.30pm and during the evening 6pm until midnight.

Kong Hans Kælder

Vingårdsstræde 6
1070 Copenhagen K
Tel. 33 11 68 68
Top-notch gourmet dining in an attractive vaulted restaurant. The **75**

wines are excellent, as are the oysters. Reservations are strongly advised. Open Monday to Saturday from 6pm until 10pm.

Krogs Fiskerestaurant

Gammel Strand 38
1202 Copenhagen K
Tel. 33 15 89 15

Located in an 18th-century building that has been fitted with early 20th-century décor, this restaurant is justly renowned for its excellent fish dishes. Reservations are recommended strongly. Open Monday to Saturday from 11.30am to 3pm and 5,30 to 10.30pm, but closed on Sunday.

Leonore Christine

Nyhavn 9
1051 Copenhagen K
Tel. 33 13 50 40

Consistently fine gourmet food, and attentive service. This restaurant is accustomed to extending an especially warm welcome to foreign visitors. Open daily noon to 3pm and 6pm until midnight.

Lumskebugten

Esplanaden 21
1263 Copenhagen K
Tel. 33 15 60 29

This small and exclusive restaurant is located by the Churchill Park near the Little Mermaid statue. Outdoor dining. Reservations are essential. Open Monday to Friday from 11am to midnight, Saturday 4pm to midnight.

Nouvelle

Gammel Strand 34
1202 Copenhagen K
Tel. 33 13 50 18

Equipped with an extensive wine cellar, sommeliers, a Michelin star and a caviar trolley, this restaurant provides an exquisite location for a special occasion. Unsurprisingly for such an establishment, prices are expensive. Reservations are essential. Open Monday to Saturday from 11.30am to midnight.

Le Pavé

Gråbrødretorv 14
1154 Copenhagen
Tel. 33 13 47 45

French-style cuisine in sophisticated surroundings. Open daily from 11.30am to midnight.

St Gertruds Kloster

Hauser Plads 32
1127 Copenhagen K
Tel. 33 14 66 30

An old monastery is the setting for this gourmet restaurant, which offers a well-stocked wine cellar and elegant menu. Reservations are strongly advised. Open daily from 5 until 11pm.

Søllerød Kro

Søllerødvej 35
2840 Holte
Tel. 42 80 25 05
Good food and a friendly atmosphere in a 17th-century inn. Outdoor dining during the summer. French cuisine with Danish flourishes. Open daily noon to 10pm.

MODERATE

A Hereford Beefstouw

Vesterbrogade 3
1620 Copenhagen V
Tel. 33 12 74 41
Juicy steaks cooked to order near Tivoli Gardens. Open daily from 11.30am to 2pm and 5 to 10pm, closed for lunch at the weekend.

Bali

Lille Kongensgade 4
1074 Copenhagen K
Tel. 33 11 08 08
On the corner of Kongens Nytorv, offering Indonesian *rijstaffel* and a selection of delicately spiced meat and vegetable dishes. Open daily from noon until midnight.

Copenhagen Corner

Rådhuspladsen
1620 Copenhagen V
Tel. 33 91 45 45
Excellent food in a restaurant that tries to maintain a traditional at-

mosphere while serving generally international cuisine. Open every day from 11.30am until midnight.

Egoisten

Hovedvagtsgade 2
1103 Copenhagen K
Tel. 33 12 79 71
Classic French food, carefully prepared. Open Monday to Saturday noon to midnight; closed Sunday.

Ginza

Gammel Kongevej 9
1610 Copenhagen V
Tel. 31 23 17 46
Stylishly presented Japanese specialities such as *sushi*. Open daily noon to 3pm and 5 to 10.30pm, closed for lunch on Sunday.

Den Gyldne Fortun

Ved Stranden 18
1061 Copenhagen K
Tel. 33 12 20 11
An established fish and shellfish restaurant. Open Monday to Friday from noon to midnight, weekends from 6pm to 10.30pm.

Hereford House

Dantes Plads 1
1556 Copenhagen V
Tel. 33 12 70 25
Standard steakhouse fare. Open Monday to Friday 11am to midnight, from midday at weekends. **77**

Nams Kusine

Strandlinien 49
Dragør
Tel. 32 53 18 18
Situated a little out of the way in the fishing village of Dragør, this delightful restaurant serves fresh seafood with an imaginative flair. The fish soup is highly recommended. Other specialities include succulent chicken roasted in a woodfired oven. Sea views add to the enjoyable culinary experience. Closed on Monday.

Peder Oxe

Gråbrødretorv 11
1154 Copenhagen K
Tel. 33 11 00 77
Excellent lunchtime *smørrebrød* offered in a restaurant with a very lively atmosphere. There is also a wine cellar. Open every day from 11.30 to 12.45am.

Rio Bravo

Vestervoldgade 86
1552 Copenhagen V
Tel. 33 11 75 87
This is a no-nonsense cowboy-style steakhouse, where even the seats at the bar are saddles! A popular restaurant, which is a firm favourite with late-night revellers. Open Monday to Saturday from 12.30pm until 4am, and Sunday from 5pm.

Spinderokken

Trommessalen 5
1614 Copenhagen V
Tel. 31 22 13 14
A typical Danish atmosphere, delightful décor and sumptuous food all combine to make a memorable dining experience. Open every day from 11.30am until 11pm.

INEXPENSIVE

Bistro DSB

Banegårdspladsen 7
1570 Copenhagen V
Tel. 33 14 12 32
This railway station restaurant offers a large cold buffet, providing a more than adequate introduction to Danish food. 11.30am to 10pm.

Bøf & Ost

Gråbrødretorv 13
1154 Copenhagen K
Tel. 33 11 99 11
French dishes served with a Danish twist. Open Monday to Saturday from 11.30am to midnight.

Café Sommersko

Kronprinsessegade 6
1114 Copenhagen
Tel. 33 14 81 89
Located just off Strøget, this is a very lively restaurant with a mixed clientele and varied menu, including numerous foreign beers. Open

Monday to Wednesday from 9 to 1am, Thursday to Saturday until 2am, and Sunday 10am to 1am.

Dhaka Town

Torvegade 60
1400 Copenhagen K
Tel. 32 96 88 01

A small, unpretentious restaurant situated close to Christianshavn Torv (bus 2 or 8 from Rådhuspladsen), specializing in Bangladeshi cuisine. Fixed-price and à la carte menus available.

Færgecaféen

Strandgade 50
1401 Copenhagen
Tel. 31 54 46 24

A little difficult to find as it is firmly tucked away in Christianshavn (buses 2 and 8), but well worth the effort. 'The Ferry', as its name translates, is a cross between a local bar and a restaurant that possesses a great deal of character. Set menu and à la carte dishes are both available.

India Palace

HC Andersens Boulevard 13
1553 Copenhagen V
Tel. 33 91 04 08, 33 91 44 08

Authentic and tasty Indian cuisine served in pleasant surroundings just a short step from Rådhuspladsen. The restaurant's delicious as-much-as-you-can-eat lunch and dinner buffets are extremely popular and excellent value. À la carte dishes also available. Open daily from 11am until midnight.

Kabul Afghansk

Studiestræde 12
1455 Copenhagen K
Tel. 33 11 11 48

The restaurant's speciality is piquant Afghan cuisine. As well as providing an unlimited buffet, it also offers à la carte dishes.

Klubben

Enghavevej 4-6
Copenhagen
Tel. 31 24 22 56

A little out of the way, but well worth a detour. A mixed menu that includes a selection of moderately priced dishes, as well as a much cheaper *smørrebrød* menu. Additional attractions include a garden terrace with fishpond and even a small bandstand.

Københavner Caféen

Badstuestræde 10
1209 Copenhagen
Tel. 33 32 80 81

A delightfully typical restaurant situated just off Strøget, which is particularly recommended for its Danish cold table. Open daily from 11am until midnight.

79

La Mexicana

Havnegade 47
1058 Copenhagen K
Tel. 33 11 32 16

A taste of tequila and tacos right in the heart of Denmark. This large restaurant offers a range of authentic cuisine in a typically Mexican atmosphere.

Mongolian Barbecue

Stormgade 35
Copenhagen
Tel. 33 14 63 20

The restaurant provides an excellent value Mongolian buffet. Open daily from 4pm until midnight.

Nyhavns Færgrekro

Nyhavn 5
1051 Copenhagen K
Tel. 33 15 15 88

An unpretentious restaurant serving particularly good traditional food. For lunch an open table with a generous array of fish is set out. Open daily 11.30am to 11.30 pm.

Pak Ka

Dronningens Tværgde 30
1302 Copenhagne K
Tel. 33 15 16 07

Cantonese cuisine in modern, airy surroundings. Dim sum is served daily (except Thursday) between 11am and 4pm. Open every day from 11am until midnight.

Riz Raz

Kompagnistræde 20
1208 Copenhagen K
Tel. 33 15 05 75

This is a Middle Eastern buffet-style restaurant, which also offers an excellent choice for vegetarians. Open daily from 11.30am until midnight.

Seoul House

Bagerstræde 9
1617 Copenhagen
Tel. 31 31 96 15

A restaurant serving Korean cuisine in a traditional setting. Open every day from noon to 3pm and evenings 6 to 10pm.

Shanghai

Nygade 6 (Strøget)
1164 Copenhagen K
Tel. 33 12 10 01

Succulent Chinese specialities at reasonable prices. Open every day from noon until 11.30pm. Also at Scala, Axeltorv 2; tel. 33 15 10 06.

Spisehuset

Rådhusstræde 13
1466 Copenhagen K
Tel. 33 14 52 70

Located in Huset, the youth centre (see p.25), the restaurant offers a cheaply priced and pleasantly varied selection of food. Open Monday to Saturday from 5pm to 1am.

NORTH ZEALAND AND ITS CASTLES

Some 115-130km (around 70-80 miles) of sea views and castle turrets, beaches and rolling farmland is what you can expect if you set about touring northern Zealand.

In fine weather you might prefer the lovely drive through the beach suburbs to the north of Copenhagen and along the so-called Danish Riviera, with its small fishing villages and bays. If you are more pushed for time, head straight up the A3 motorway (or expressway) out of Copenhagen in the direction of Helsingør.

One major attraction just to the south of Humlebæk, accessible from either the A3 or the coast road, is the **Louisiana Modern Art Museum** which is housed in the mid-19th-century mansion of a thrice-married cheese merchant whose wives were all called Louise. The superb gardens are dotted with sculptures ranging from chunky Henry Moore works to metal mobiles by Alexander Calder. The airy, white interior houses everything from mural-sized Chagalls to special pop-art shows. Open all year round Monday to Friday 10am-5pm, also till 10pm on Wednesday, 10am-6pm weekends.

The **castle** at **Helsingør** (to many of us better known as Elsinore) soon appears within view, jutting out towards the

Outside at the Louisiana Museum you can admire works on show or just enjoy the view.

direction of Sweden, a striking square of green roofs standing against the blue Sound.

'Hamlet's castle' is a misnomer, of course. Though Laurence Olivier and Vivien Leigh certainly trod its ancient corridors when making the film of *Hamlet*, the tragic prince himself never slept here and it is probable anyway that Shakespeare derived the name from Amleth (or Amled), a Jutland prince of pre-Viking times.

The real name of the castle is Kronborg. It was built between 1574 and 1585 at the command of King Frederik II for the purpose of extracting-tolls from ships that were entering the narrow Sound (and thus the Baltic) at this point.

Frederik had more than just a stronghold in mind. He built a castle that could be lived in, so fortified with ramparts and bastions that a number of large windows and decorated towers could be added with impunity. He sent for Flemish architect Antonius van Opbergen to design the four-wing structure and then engaged various Danish and Dutch artists to paint,

weave and indulge in decorative sculpture on a scale never before seen in Scandinavia.

Restored this century, today the moated brick castle stands as Frederik's proudest memorial, now sparsely furnished but immensely impressive. It has a feel of solid strength and royal presence throughout, permeating the elaborate little **chapel**, the long galleries and the stone stairways, and most of all the huge oak-beamed **Banqueting Hall**. At 64m by 11m (210ft by 36ft), it is the largest hall of its kind in northern Europe and one of the noblest rooms of the Danish Renaissance. Decked out now with twelve paintings of the Sound by Isaac Isaacsz, its white walls were once hung with 42 famous tapestries by the Dutchman Hans Knieper, depicting the 111 Danish kings said to have reigned before Frederik II. Fourteen of the tapestries still survive, of which

From afar, Kronborg Castle is a striking sight – at close quarters its grace is also evident.

*B*attles played out on the castle's tapestries contrast with the peace of cottages at Helsingør.

In the castle's northern wing you'll discover the interesting **Handels- og Søfartsmuseet** (Trade and Maritime Museum) with its display of navigation instruments, as well as relics from early Danish settlements in Greenland and elsewhere.

The castle and museum are open daily except Mondays, May-September 10am-5pm, November-March 11am-3pm, April and October 11am-4pm; guided tours every half-hour.

After perhaps stopping for a coffee at one of the numerous cafés on Helsingør's 18th-century market place, keep going along the northern coast road to Dronningmølle, which has one of the best beaches on the Kattegat, before turning south in the direction of Esrum for a cross-sectional view of rural Zealand: winding lanes, beech forests, farmland cultivated to the road edge, and traditional farmsteads that are built with four wings surrounding a cobbled courtyard. At Esrum, follow the signs via Jonstrup and drive along the Esrum Sø to the castle lying on the water's edge, **Fredensborg Slot**.

seven are to be seen in a small room beneath the hall, and the remainder in the National Museum (see p.56). Underneath the castle are extensive casements and dungeons. The most famous exhibit at Kronborg, however, is the statue of Holger the Dane (see p.8).

84

Erected between 1719 and 1722, Fredensborg is an excellent example of Italian/Dutch baroque, set on a small hill, surrounded by grounds that were the delight of King Frederik V, who turned this hunting seat into a royal summer residence. He held great parties here, and had statues installed in the lakeside grounds – not of his peers but of ordinary people, with exact renderings of the folk costumes. You can stroll the grounds any time, but the royal apartments and the private garden are open only in the royal family's absence.

Continue for a further 9km (5½ miles) as far as Hillerød and the site of Denmark's architectural showpiece, Christian IV's grandest achievement, and one of the greatest Renaissance castles in northern Europe: **Frederiksborg Slot**, a brick and sandstone castle dramatically sited across three islands. During the years of the absolutist kings, every single Danish monarch was anointed and crowned here.

85

In 1859 much of the interior was destroyed by fire. Twenty years later a plan put forward by the brewer JC Jacobsen to restore the castle into a Danish Versailles – a museum of national history – was approved by royal ordinance. Spanning more than 60 rooms of the castle, there is today a complete record of the Danish monarchy, begining with Christian I who established the Oldenburg line (1448-1863), through all the monarchs of the following Glücksburg line, right down to the present queen.

*P*ause for wonder at Frederiksborg Castle – or has the guide just forgotten those lines?

Riddersalen (the Knights' Hall) and the chapel are Frederiksborg's ultimate triumph. The 56m (185ft) Knights' Hall is awesome in its dimensions, with tapestried walls, marble floor and carved wooden ceiling, all reconstructed from old drawings after the 1859 fire.

Below the Knights' Hall, **Slotskirken** (the chapel) escaped the fire with its stunning gilt pillars and high vaulted nave virtually untouched. Almost every inch here is richly carved and ornamented. The chapel has inset black marble panels with scriptural quotes, marquetry panels in ebony and rare woods, and both its altar and pulpit in ebony with biblical scenes in silver relief. The **organ** is one of Europe's most notable, an almost unchanged original from 1610 by Flemish master Esaias Compenius.

Around the gallery of this wondrous chapel the window piers and recesses are all hung with coats-of-arms belonging to Knights of both the Order of the Elephant and Order of the Grand Cross of Dannebrog. If you look around, you'll also spot some modern recipients, such as Sir Winston Churchill and General Eisenhower.

After a short stroll around the cobbled courtyards, perhaps pausing for a rest beside the 1620 **Neptune Fountain**, return to Copenhagen, 32km (20mile) back along the A5.

Frederiksborg Castle stays open every day all year round: April 10am-4pm, May-September 10am-5pm, October 10am-4pm, November-March 11am-3pm. Without a car, it can be independently reached by regular S-train service to Hillerød; then from the centre of Hillerød the Frederiksborg Ferry plies across the lake towards the castle. Sightseeing tours starting from Copenhagen are also available during most of the year.

ROSKILDE

With an 800-year-old cathedral housing the splendid tombs of 37 monarchs, with Viking ships salvaged from the fjord and now presented in a unique maritime museum, with young scientists welcoming visitors to their nearby prehistoric village, Roskilde has plenty to offer those who undertake the brief (30-minute) journey from Copenhagen centre.

Whether you go by car, bus or train, make straight for the centre of this small, neat town and for the three green spires **87** which dominate the flat landscape for miles about. This is **Domkirken** (the Cathedral), begun as a wooden church by King Harald Bluetooth around 1000 when he was converted to Christianity. In the 1170s, Bishop Absalon, founder of Copenhagen (see p.9), built a brick and stone cathedral here for his new bishopric, and during the course of the next 300 years this grew into the Romanesque-Gothic amalgam of today. Christian IV added the distinctive spires in 1635. He also erected his own burial chapel and a gilded royal pew in the north wall of the church, heavily latticed and shielded from public view so that (it is said) he could smoke his pipe in peace during Sunday services. Nearly all the Danish kings and queens since Margrete (d. 1412) are buried here.

The sarcophagi and chapels are all different from one another, a jumbled symphony of style. On the south side, the chapel of King Frederik V is simple in white paint and Norwegian marble, with 12 tombs grouped around it. In contrast, the Christian IV chapel on the north side is marked by elaborately wrought ironwork from 1618 and interior decoration mainly in the 19th century.

A light note is introduced by the clock high on the southwest wall of the nave. As each hour arrives, St George and his horse rear up, beneath them a dragon utters a shrill cry, and a woman figure strikes her little bell four times with a hammer, a man his big bell once.

The chapel on the outside of the cathedral beside the north-western tower was inaugurated in 1985 and dedicated to the memory of Frederik IX, King of Denmark from 1947 to 1972, who is buried there.

To the front of the church is Stændertorvet, the traditional square of this old market town, lined with outdoor café tables in good weather, and fruit and vegetable stalls every Wednesday and Saturday morning. On Saturday there is also a popular flea market. To the rear is some public parkland, where you can walk down to the fjord and **Vikingeskibshallen** (the Viking Ship Museum).

When 11th-century Danes wanted to block off the sea-route to Roskilde from the ravaging Norwegians, they sank five Viking ships across a narrow neck of the shallow fjord here. These ships, salvaged in 1962, now form the basis of the Viking Ship Museum. The museum building stands on the edge of the water with one side completely glass, bringing the fjord almost into its room. The outline of each ship was first reconstructed in metal strips, then the thousands of pieces of wood were placed in position after specialist treatment.

The museum is lavishly illustrated with photographs and charts, and free film shows are put on for the public in the cinema-cellar, recounting the full story of the salvage in English.

Rescued from the sea-bed, these Viking ships are now carefully looked after near the site of their watery graves at Roskilde.

89

*V*isible for miles, the spire of Roskilde Domkirke has stood firm through many centuries.

Roskilde is a go-ahead town offering lively entertainment, with open-air theatre and fjord boat trips in summer, concerts and cattle shows, bonfires and fireworks. If you are going by train, ask at Copenhagen Station for the special Roskilde ticket (*Roskilde særtilbud*), a package including entrance to the cathedral and ship museum as well as your return rail fare.

Continue 10km (6 miles) south-west, by Lejre, to reach the Historical-Archaeological Research Centre **Oldtidsbyen** (Ancient Town). Here a group of enthusiasts are not only living in Iron-Age style, in clay and reed houses that look like a cluster of shaggy dogs, but are actually in the throes of a major long-term scientific experiment in which they are attempting to trace the effect on the environment of primitive man's use of tools, examining how his needs and life-style destroyed or amended the natural amenities, how forest and wildlife disappeared, etc.

Every year 80,000 visitors flock to Lejre to see the animal farm, the workshops, the explanatory film shows in Danish and English and for a peep into the curiously reincarnated prehistoric houses with their smoky interiors and primitive living conditions.

The village is open April-September daily 10am-5pm; but is closed in winter.

What to Do

Shopping

Shopping in Copenhagen is a quality experience, and the city's pedestrianized precincts and attractive squares add to the pleasure of seeking out that special purchase. A host of interesting shops in the pleasant side streets and shopping arcades around the Strøget area specialize in everything from antiques to avant-garde furniture, while established department stores such as Illum and Magasin du Nord offer the very best in Danish design.

SHOPPING HOURS

Shops are generally open from 9.30 or 10am until 5.30pm, Monday to Friday. Late-night shopping hours extend to 7pm on Friday, and sometimes also on Thursday. A small number of shops (often food shops) are closed on Monday or Tuesday, and on Saturday hours are 9am to noon or 2pm, with the exception of the first Saturday in the month when doors usually close at 5pm.

Certain shops around town remain open outside normal shopping hours. These include bakeries, florists, *smørrebrød* shops, sweet shops and kiosks.

In addition, late-night (until 10pm or midnight) and Sunday shopping is possible at the Central Station, which is like a cheery village with a 24-hour heel bar, a supermarket, banks open for foreign exchange, a post office, room-booking service and snack bars.

There are several central 24-hour shops (look for the sign *dag og nat shop*) selling fresh bread from 3am onwards plus other food, beer and spirits.

WHERE TO SHOP

The linked, completely pedestrianized streets of Strøget/Fiolstræde/Købmagergade have it all: the finest ceramics and silver shops, perhaps the greatest art-household stores in the world, the city's leading furriers, antique shops by the score (also found in some smaller streets branching off), workshops belonging to young potters and silversmiths, shops for clothes and knitwear, toys and pipes, and dozens of souvenir shops and kiosks.

Slightly more off the beaten track – unless you're visiting Amalienborg and the Marble Church – is Bredgade/Store Kongensgade, with its extensive range of boutiques.

Sales tax, or VAT (in Danish MOMS), is 25 per cent on all products and services. This tax will be refunded to foreign visitors who make large purchases (above 600kr) in outlets that display 'Tax-Free Shopping' stickers. Ask for details in the shop. (See also p.130.)

GOOD BUYS

Amber jewellery is on offer everywhere, particularly in the shops along Strøget. The local 'gem' (actually fossil resin), from the southern Baltic, may be cheaper here than at home.

Antiques are in plentiful supply, especially the home-spun

*E*ach one different: the meticulous and painstaking workmanship of the porcelain factory.

rather than the fine-art variety. The most likely shops to try are in the old town area.

Aquavit (*akvavit*) is the local spirit, usually flavoured with caraway seed, and is cheaper than imported spirits. The best prices are at airport duty-free.

Danish porcelain. The secret of its poetic effect is an underglaze technique shared only by Royal Copenhagen Porcelain (founded in 1775) and Bing & Grøndahl (1853) which allows landscape pastels, and even accurate skin colours, to be reproduced. Blue motifs come out particularly well. All the pieces from these companies are hand-painted after a quick first firing, then fired again for glazing at 1,400°C (2,600°F). No two pieces are alike. They range from ashtrays to dinner services, with prices to match.

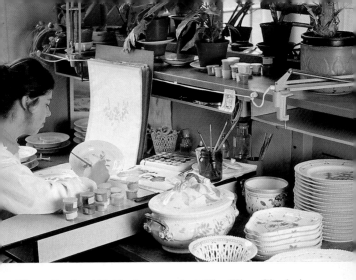

The stylized and highly decorative ceramics of the contemporary Danish artist Bjørn Wiinblad are highly popular, while avant-garde and classic European designs are available from Rosenthal Studio-Haus at Frederiksberggade 21 near Rådhuspladsen.

Glassware and **stainless steel** household products are especially good buys to take home if you want top quality design matched with excellent craftsmanship. There is still a thriving tradition of blown glass, and at Hinz/Kjær Glasdesign in Pistolstræde you can watch skilled craftsmen at work on their exquisite and colourful creations.

Stereo equipment. The very latest in stereo systems, CD players, radios and TV sets can be found at the Bang & Olufsen Center, Østergade 3-5, near to Kongens Nytorv.

Household furnishings. Danish furniture ranks among the world's best. Here you'll see items credited to the designer **93**

rather than to the factory. Furniture is a national pride and most good pieces will have a black circular 'Danish Furniture-Makers' Control' sticker attached. Lamps are also a lovingly designed product, as are household textiles and hand-woven rugs. The best shops for interior furnishings are Illums Bolighus on Strøget and Tre Falke Møbler in the Falkoner Centre on Falkoner Allé. Look out, too, for traditional Danish eiderdowns and duvets; Ofelia in Strøget Arcade off Vimmel-

skaftet offers an excellent and varied selection.

Knitwear comes Nordic-style, often highly patterned, warm and in some cases expensive. Knitwear shops are dotted all over the city; some sell wool and patterns for those who are tempted to set about knitting their own garments.

Silver is another Danish speciality, dominated by the name Georg Jensen. Silver in Denmark is quality-controlled and should always be hallmarked. The Jensen showrooms at Amagertorv 4 offer creations that range from key rings to highly precious jewellery.

Souvenirs are myriad. Little mermaid figures, Copenhagen dolls in frilly skirts and black lace caps, ceramic blue figurines and animals and countless kinds of trolls and Vikings abound, as well as hand-painted spoons, racks and peppermills. A particularly attractive Danish keepsake is an Amager shelf – a group of three or four small hand-painted shelves in a triangular frame that hangs on the wall. Beware, however, of cheap versions.

Toys are simple and attractive, especially those in solid wood. You'll also see hundreds of the Danish wooden soldiers in all sizes. Many new shops such as Krea have opened up which specialize in educational toys for children of all ages.

Entertainment

When in Copenhagen, relax as the Danes do. Hire a bike for a different view of life, stroll the beech woods and parks, have a night on the town at a concert or jazz club – or simply pause for a snack on one of the many public benches.

Beaches. Bellevue Beach is a mere 20 minutes journey away by S-train (line C) to Klampenborg – so easy, you'll join in a city exodus on sunny days.

Botanical gardens. Keen gardeners could happily pass two or three days examining the 70 laid-out areas, the palm house and various other greenhouses on the 10ha (25 acre) Botanisk Have site opposite Rosenborg Castle. It remains open year-round till sunset. Get there by bus 14 from Rådhuspladsen, or alternatively buses 7 and 17 from Kongens Nytorv.

Café society. Another way of life altogether – relaxed, welcoming. Sit as long as you like

Behind glass windows, or on the streets, there's always music in the making in Copenhagen.

You can buy last minute tickets at half price for performances at Copenhagen's Royal Theatre.

over a beer or coffee, let yourself gaze at the eccentric décor and take time out to meet the Danes. There are several especially friendly bars in the area of the University.

Cycling. Some hotels lend bicycles free to their guests. Otherwise they're easy to hire (see p.116). Once you're perched on a saddle, the world is your oyster. Ride the extensive network of cycle paths (*cykelsti*) without any worry about cars, or indeed the weather – if it decides to rain, country buses will pack your bike on the top. Taxis also have bicycle racks.

NIGHTLIFE

Music, opera, ballet: scores of concerts are held all year at the Royal Theatre, Tivoli, the Royal Conservatory of Music, Radio House, in churches and in museums. The Royal Danish Ballet is world-renowned, and rightly so; it is one of Europe's oldest, with a 200-year-old repertory. Nowadays, the company experiments in modern dance as well, but its great tradition is Bournonville classics, which are worth trying to go to see. The Ballet performs from September to June only.

Jazz, **folk**, **rock**: Copenhagen has been called Europe's leading jazz centre. Various main clubs offer jazz for all persuasions every night till 2am or later. Many foreign stars now live in Denmark and appear at leading clubs, like Club Montmartre in Nørregade. At smaller bars the jazz is free. There are four venues for folk music in the downtown area near the University. Rock music events frequently appear in the regular Copenhagen listings. Free rock concerts on summer Sundays are held in Fælled Park.

Festivals

Denmark has no great religious festivals or processions, few spectacular state ceremonies. Yet festivities of some kind are in the air all the time, and a glance at *Copenhagen This Week* (see p.128) will give you an idea of just how many. The following summary gives a flavour of what to expect during the year:

St John's Eve: *Sankt Hansaften* (June 23). Bonfires are lit all along the 'Riviera' coastline north of Copenhagen to drive the witches away on their broomsticks to Blocksberg in Germany.

Viking Festival: *Vikingespil* (mid-June to early July). Plays, mead and barbecues at Frederikssund (bus tours available).

Copenhagen Summer Festival: Pop concerts and chamber music in different parts of the city; admission is free.

Roskilde Festival: (late June to early July). Greatest pop festival in northern Europe – jazz and rock in a delightful setting.

Copenhagen Jazz Festival: (mid July). International jazz.

Copenhagen Choir Festival: (late October). Choral events.

Now in glorious techni-colour! The facade of one of a number of cinema complexes.

Nightclubs: there is a plethora of late-opening bars that serve as nightclubs, with the emphasis firmly on entertainment.

Discos: the usual routine is to enrol as a member at the door. Almost everything from downbeat discotheques to sophisticated hotel nightclubs.

Cinemas: films are shown in their original language together with Danish subtitles.

At home: if you are fortunate enough to be invited to a Danish home, make sure you grab the chance. The Danes love to entertain and set great store by creating a cosy yet chic atmosphere for their guests.

Copenhagen by night: Copenhagen is, of course, well known for its more risqué entertainment and red-light district. This is now located in the less obtrusive Istedgade/Halmtorvet area to the west of the Central Station.

Sports

There's plenty for every type within easy reach of the city. Top spectator sport is football (soccer), while popular participation sports are sailing and fishing. Ask the nearest Danish tourist office (see p.135) for an up-to-date list of all facilities, or contact the Copenhagen Sports Centre (Idrættens Hus), tel. 42 45 55 55.

Bungee jumping. This daring activity has recently taken off

98

internationally, and in Copenhagen you can practise it in the safety of the harbour.

Fishing. Jutland is the Danish mecca for sea fishing, but you can still go for Øresund cod, mackerel, gar-pike or flat-fish from Amager and the coast to the north of the city. No special permit is required for fishing in Denmark, either in its lakes or rivers – a real boost to anglers. You can hire licensed boats on Lyngby, Furesø and Bagsværd lakes on the northwest edge of Copenhagen.

Football (soccer). The Danish football team competes at the highest level, and the sport has an enthusiastic following. Amateur games are played every weekend from April to June and August to November, and certain weekday afternoons in May, June and September. The main Copenhagen stadium is at Idrætsparken.

Woken by sunshine, the campers and holiday-makers of Denmark prepare for a new day.

Golf. With at least 30 clubs in Denmark, and 8 within 40km (25 miles) of Copenhagen, the nearest being in Klampenborg suburb at Dyrehaven 2, tel. 31 63 04 83, golf is always an option. Green fees are moderate throughout Denmark, and foreigners are welcomed.

Horse-racing. Also located at Klampenborg, the racing track (*galopbane*) opens mainly Saturdays from mid-April to mid-December. Take the S-train to Klampenborg, then bus 160.

Riding. Good riding, especially in the Deer Park. There are several stables and schools in the area; for details look in the *Fagbog* (a telephone directory to trade and professions) under *Rideundervisning*.

Rowing. A major sporting activity, with an Olympic course and many clubs – details available from the Danish Rowing Association (*Dansk Forening for Rosport*), Vester Voldgade 91, 1552 Copenhagen V.

Sailing. Join the Sound and inland lake throngs. Yachts and cruisers are available for hire. Evidence of navigational proficiency is required for sailing on the Øresund, where a close watch must be kept out for the constant ferry traffic. Book in advance with help from your local Danish tourist office.

Skating. Numerous stretches of water within the city boundaries freeze up in winter. There are also indoor rinks (*skøjtehal*) at Copenhagen Forum and other suburban locations. All open October-April.

Swimming. There is good sea bathing along the whole of the Zealand coast north and south of the city, but the sea is rarely warm. Nude bathing is mainly at Tisvildeleje, away from the north coast. There are about a dozen indoor swimming baths in Copenhagen, some of these with sauna/massage and gym facilities, and several outdoor pools which open from mid-May until end August.

Tennis. For a small fee, you can obtain guest membership of local clubs. Foreign players are welcome, though advance booking is necessary. Contact the tourist office for addresses.

Watersports. Water-skiing is popular on the Furesø, and it is possible to windsurf in Vedbæk harbour; contact Vedbæk Surf School and Hire, tel. 45 76 74 05, or try consulting the tourist office for details.

*P*ractising on the river, left; a pensive bungee jumper awaits her turn in the harbour.

Children's Copenhagen

Amusement parks. Tivoli, of course, should certainly appeal to the whole family. Another really fun place for children is **Bakken**, 10km (6 miles) north of Copenhagen on the edge of the Deer Park. It's older than Tivoli and slightly less sophisticated, with a big dipper and beer hall, circus revue and hall of distorting mirrors, a bingo and pantomime, a children's play park (look for *børnelegeplads*), funfairs, dodgems and a wide choice of eating establishments: while you are here take the opportunity to try the *æbleskiver som vor mor bager dem*, 'apple slices like mother makes' (deep-fried in batter). Open during the summer; entrance is free.

Circus. Lying almost opposite Tivoli, down Axeltorv. Established in 1887 and voted the best circus in continental Europe for four years in a row. It holds shows every night, from May to October.

Dyrehaven. To one side of the rail station for Bellevue Beach, you'll find the entrance to the Royal Deer Park, now open to all and stretching for miles. Go along by horse and carriage to watch the deer feeding. Make sure, however, to check carefully on the prices.

Museums and attractions. A likely hit with the children is **Ripley's Believe it or Not!** museum at Rådhuspladsen 57, a motley collection of 'bizarre but true' exhibits including a shrunken head. Other favourite children's attractions include: the **Tycho Brahe** Planetarium, Gammel Kongevej 10, with its space theatre and star shop; the **Ecksperimentarium** science centre, Tuborg Havnevej 7, Hellerup, where the kids are positively encouraged to tinker around with exhibits; and the **Aquarium**, Charlottenlund, a home to more than 3,000 varieties of aquatic life, including bloodthirsty piranhas.

Tours. Almost anything to do with water appeals to youngsters, and organized canal trips

*F*rom a Legoland perspective, adults are just a crowd. The extraordinary miniature world here has always proved a popular destination.

are a must. Also worth considering are the boat cruises that depart from Roskilde harbour west of the city. Among farther-flung options are a coach tour to **Legoland** in Jutland, and a train journey to **Fantasy World** in South Zealand, with the chance thrown in to catch a glimpse of Santa Claus. Contact the tourist office for details of these and other tours.

Zoo. Copenhagen's Zoologisk Have is one of the finest in Europe, and has been around for over 120 years. It plays host to more than 2,500 animals, and has a splendid children's section, restaurant and cafeteria. It is open all year from 9am to sunset or to 6pm at the latest: Roskildevej 32, and only a 10-minute ride from Rådhuspladsen by buses 28 and 41.

Eating Out

Food is of a high standard in Denmark, and counts as little short of an obsession. Danes at home will happily spend two hours over their *frokost* (lunch) or up to four if entertaining special guests, whilst a dinner (*middag*) in celebratory mood can last from 6pm to infinity.

Restaurants and Bars

There are more than 2,000 assorted restaurants, cafés, bars and snack bars in Copenhagen. Restaurants often serve a special dish of the day (*dagens ret*) and what is known as the 'Dan-menu' – a two-course Danish lunch or dinner for a fixed price – in addition to à la carte items. Keep an eye open for a *daglig kort* ('daily card') which usually features less expensive dishes than those listed on the more formal menu (*spisekort*). You'll also find little lunch-only, cosy cellar restaurants listed in *Copenhagen This Week* (see p.128). These offer good value, with an old-world charm, and are well frequented by Danes themselves. Out of town, a *kro* (country inn) can provide a charming if occasionally expensive setting for a special meal.

For a drink in the evening (or in fact practically any time of the day or night – opening hours are particularly liberal), drop into one of the numerous cafés, pubs or bars that are dotted throughout the city. One traditional Danish drinking establishment is the *værtshus*, which will be tidy or tatty according to its neighbourhood.

Value-added tax and service charge are included in the bill. Danes are not tip-minded, although after a meal you may want to round up your bill.

Breakfast

Breakfast (*morgenmad*) in a Danish hotel is a far cry from the Spartan 'continental breakfast' of a roll and a cup of coffee. Bread rolls, meat, cheese, jam, pastries and possibly an egg are all accompanied by a glass of milk or fruit juice followed by tea or coffee.

Cold Dishes

Cold food is Denmark's truly outstanding culinary speciality, which you can soon learn to enjoy. *Smørrebrød* are thickly buttered slices of rye or white bread covered with one of a wide array of delicacies: liver paté (*leverpostej*), beef tartare (*bøf tartar*), veal (*kalvekød*), ham (*skinke*), roast beef (*roast beef*), salmon (*laks*), smoked eel (*røget ål*), shrimps (*rejer*), cod-roe (*torskerogn*), herring (*sild*), salad (*salat*) or cheese (*ost*). This main layer is garnished with a variety of accessories that have been carefully chosen to enhance both taste and appearance. Larger restaurants have scores of different *smørrebrød*. The usual procedure is to tick off your orders on the menu itself, specifying which kind of bread you want

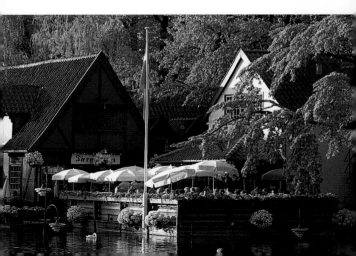

*A*fternoon draws on, while lunch follows its leisurely course at Tivoli Gardens' Ferry Inn.

Skål! ...and tak!

Learn to say *skål* (the vowel is between 'loll' and 'hall') with your beer or *akvavit*. It's more than just Danish for 'cheers' – it's a ritual if you are invited to a Danish home. Your host usually has privilege of first toast, and will raise a glass, point it towards everyone in turn, looking directly at them – and say *skål*. After all have taken a sip or a swallow, the host will look at each again in turn before putting down the glass.

After the meal itself, the appropriate – and essential – thing to say is *tak for mad* (which is pronounced 'tak for maad'), meaning, very simply, 'thanks for the meal'.

(*knækbrød*: crispbread; *rugbrød*: rye; *franskbrød*: white; *pumpernikkel*: black). Two or three of these substantial 'open sandwiches' will generally satisfy most appetites. However, just to give you an idea, one Copenhagen restaurant offers 178 varieties of *smørrebrød*.

Don't confuse your *smørrebrød* with the Swedish word *smörgåsbord* which has gained international currency as a description of the pan-Scandinavian cold buffet-style spread, better known in Denmark as the *koldt bord* ('cold table'). Larger restaurants especially will offer a bewildering array of dishes in their *koldt bord*. For a fixed price, you start at one end of the table helping yourself to herring in various preparations, seafood, mayonnaise salads and other delicacies, and go on to sample liver paté, ham and other cuts of meat. Despite its name, a *koldt bord* always includes a few hot items, such as meat balls, pork sausages, soup and fried potatoes. Several kinds of bread and salads are also provided.

En platte is a cold dish (a smaller version of *koldt bord*) made up of six to eight specialities, which is often eaten at lunchtime. Danish *akvavit* (see p.110) and beer go especially well with a *koldt bord*.

Fish and Shellfish

Fish (or small canapés) is the traditional first course of a full meal. It is also available individually, of course, and a great variety of fish appear on the Danish menu. **Herring** is one of the firm favourites, and may be served pickled, marinated or fried, with a sherry, vinegar, curry or fennel dressing. Succulent red Greenland **shrimps** are also very popular. Lobster is widely on offer – though it is not cheap – as are crab, cod and halibut.

Plaice features frequently in the local cuisine and may be served boiled or fried with a garnish of shellfish or parsley. You'll see the little Øresund *rødspætte* (red-spot plaice) on every menu. In summer, a speciality is *danske rejer*, small pink shrimps from local waters that are served piled high on white bread.

Eel is a speciality during the winter months, when it is usually fried and served in a white sauce alongside creamy boiled potatoes and lashings of sliced lemon; or alternatively, salted eel may be boiled and served with horseradish.

One great Scandinavian delicacy is **gravad laks**, in which raw salmon is pressed with salt

F resh seafood of every kind, about to be devoured in a sky-line restaurant above the city.

and a small amount of sugar, and then sprinkled generously with chopped dill; a cold sauce of oil, mustard and sugar is traditionally served alongside as an accompaniment.

A street café on Kongens Nytorv, near to the Royal Theatre and Nyhavn.

The best fish restaurants in Copenhagen are to be found in the Gammel Strand area.

Meat and Poultry

Although Danish meat dishes most frequently make use of **pork** and **veal**, **beef** has made a major breakthrough as Danish farmers now breed more cattle. Note that **lamb** is available only from May to September. The kinds of steak that you are most likely to be offered are *fransk bøf*, fillet steak served with herb butter and chips (French fries), and *engelsk bøf*, fillet steak served with fried onions and potatoes.

The top restaurants cook in classic French style. In small establishments, however, some typical Danish hot dishes remain; *mørbradbøf* is a delectable legacy of the pork-only days – small steaks of what is called tenderloin in English, lean, very tasty and served as a main course with boiled potatoes, onions and gravy.

For more ordinary fare – but tasty nevertheless – try Danish meatballs (*frikadeller*), a finely minced mixture of pork and veal, often served with potato salad and red cabbage. *Bikse-mad* is also cheap and tasty: a Danish hash of diced potatoes, meat and onions with a fried egg on top. *Hakkebøf* is the crumbling Danish hamburger, while *pariserbøf* is a slightly cooked, almost raw, hamburger topped with egg yolk, raw onion, capers, and horseradish. A hearty Danish stew is *Hvids labskovs*, made from chunks of beef boiled with potatoes, peppercorns and bay leaves.

Chicken is most frequently served roasted with potatoes fried in butter and a cucumber salad (*agurkesalat*). **Turkey** is less commonly found on Danish menus, but may be served roasted or boiled as one of a selection of lunchtime dishes. Roast **duck** comes with apple or prune stuffing and is usually accompanied by caramelized potatoes and a generous array of vegetables.

Salads

The word for salad, *salat*, has two meanings. It can be the fa-miliar side-dish of fresh lettuce, tomato, sliced egg, and plentiful red peppers; or, more often, it's one of several mayonnaise mixtures that are eaten on *smørrebrød* or as an appetizer. *Italiensk salat* consists of diced carrots, asparagus, peas and macaroni. *Skinkesalat* is basically chopped ham, while *sildesalat* comprises marinated or pickled herring, beetroot, apple and pickles. These are only the most common of numerous sandwich salads generally available.

Cheese and Fruit

Danish Blue (*Danablu*), a rich, sharp-flavoured cheese, has always had a strong international following. *Mycella* is fairly similar in taste, but is milder. *Fynbo* and *Samsø* are both relatively mild and firm cheeses and possess a sweetish, almost nutty flavour.

Fruit will always come after the cheese platter if you're eating out. Although the greater part of the country's fruit is imported, Denmark can boast a wide range of berries.

109

Desserts

It will have been obvious from the very start that Denmark is not a good place for dieting. And by the time you get your Danish desserts your best intentions will have been quite definitely routed! Your dessert will almost certainly be laced with cream (*fløde*) or whipped cream (*flødeskum*).

Favourite desserts include: *æblekage* (stewed apples with vanilla, served with alternating layers of biscuit crumbs and topped with whipped cream); also, *bondepige med slør* (a mixture of rye-bread crumbs, apple sauce, sugar and that ubiquitous whipped cream).

Snacks

For a snack with a difference, try the deep-fried Camembert cheese served with toast and strawberry jam (*ristet franskbrø med friturestegt camembert og jordbærsyltetøj*).

The university area is good for cheap goulashes, hashes, chicken and *håndmadder* (usually three slender *smørrebrød*

with different toppings). Hot-dog stands (*pølsevogn*) may be found everywhere, serving red Danish sausages (*pølse*) with mustards and relishes.

Oddly enough, Danish pastry is known as Viennese pastry (*wienerbrød*) in Denmark. This distinctive light and flaky delight can be found in any *konditori*, and makes a delectable snack in the middle of the morning or afternoon.

Drinks

Golden Danish **lager** comes in several types: *lys pilsner* (light lager) which has only 2 per cent alcohol; the more normal green-bottle *pilsner*; and finally the stouts and special beers (like *elefantøl*) at 6-7 per cent or more. *Pilsner* is available everywhere almost 24 hours a day. In cafés it costs three or four times the shop price. The rarer draught beer (*fadøl*) is less fizzy and slightly cheaper.

Akvavit is the fiery Danish schnaps, made from potatoes, and often with a caraway taste. The colour varies according to the herbs and spices that have been used for flavouring. It is taken at mealtimes during the opening fish course or with the cheese, and will sometimes be washed down with a beer chaser. If you order *akvavit* with your meal, the bottle may occasionally be put on the table for you to help yourself. Don't be deluded into thinking you'll only be charged for a single measure – back in the bar they will know exactly how much has gone.

There is also an increasingly popular **non-alcoholic beer**, which has recently been introduced, looking and tasting like pilsner and costing the same.

All **wines** are imported, and while there is a wide selection of French, German and Italian varieties, they are always reasonably expensive in restaurants. Even cheap house-wine (*husets vin*) may be three times the supermarket price. After your dinner, try Danish cherry liqueur, *Cherry Heering*.

Coffee (*kaffe*) can be found everywhere, rich, strong and served with cream. The price may seem high, but the waiter will usually come round offering refills. On a chilly day you might like to try *varm kakao med flødeskum* – a hot cocoa with whipped cream.

Beer, Bottles and Cans

Beer, *øl* (draught beer is called *fadøl*), is rather expensive in Denmark, but it is much cheaper when purchased from a retail outlet. Supermarkets and other stores are open until 5.30pm on weekdays and 2pm on Saturday, although some smaller shops do stay open until 8 or 9pm during the week. Technically, it is illegal to sell beer outside these hours and on Sunday and public holidays, though some of the smaller shops turn a blind eye to the law. Don't expect to see cans; for environmental reasons, these are not used in Denmark. Remember there is a deposit for each bottle, which may be refunded by any store.

To Help You Order ...

Could we have a table?	**Må vi få et bord?**
Do you have a set menu?	**Har De en dagens ret?**
I'd like a/an/some ...	**Jeg vil gerne have ...**

beer	**en øl**	napkin	**en serviet**
bread	**brød**	pepper	**peber**
coffee	**kaffe**	potatoes	**kartofler**
dessert	**en dessert**	salad	**en salat**
fish	**fisk**	salt	**salt**
glass	**et glas**	soup	**suppe**
ice-cream	**is**	sugar	**sukker**
meat	**kød**	tea	**te**
menu	**et spisekort**	vegetables	**grønsager**
milk	**mælk**	(iced) water	**(is) vand**
mustard	**sennep**	wine	**vin**

...and Read the Menu

agurkesalat	cucumber salad	**kål**	cabbage
blomkål	cauliflower	**lagkage**	layer cake
citron	lemon	**lever**	liver
flæskesteg	roast pork and crackling	**løg**	onion
		medisterpølse	pork sausage
grøn peber	green pepper	**nyrer**	kidney
grønne bønner	french beans	**oksekød**	beef
gulerødder	carrots	**pommes frites**	french fries
hamburgerryg	loin of pork	**porrer**	leeks
hindbær	raspberries	**rødkål**	red cabbage
jordbær	strawberries	**svinekød**	pork
kartoffelmos	mashed potatoes	**søtunge**	sole
kirsebær	cherries	**æble**	apple
kotelet	chop	**æg**	egg
kylling	chicken	**æggekage**	omelette

112

BLUEPRINT
for a
Perfect Trip

An A–Z Summary of Practical Information

ACCOMMODATION (*hotel; indlogering*)
(See also CAMPING on p.116, YOUTH HOSTELS on p.139, and the list of RECOMMENDED HOTELS starting on p.66)
Danish tourist offices will provide you with extensive lists of hotels and pensions. There is no star-system of rating, but the lists give an indication of various facilities (with bath, restaurant, number of beds, etc). Combine this information with the prices listed, and you get a fair indication of quality. Ask your tourist office, too, for details of special low rates in off-season. They can be down by as much as 50%. Rates on p.131 are averages for double rooms in high season. Service charges and taxes are included. Single rooms are generally about 30-40% cheaper.

If you arrive in Copenhagen without a room, try the room-booking service at the tourist information centre, Bernstorffsgade 1, tel. 33 12 28 80, fax 33 12 97 23; expect to pay a small fee. Even at peak holiday periods the Accommodation Bureau, Kiosk P, at the Central Railway Station rarely fails to find room for all. The bureau is open daily from 9am to midnight between May and mid-September, and till 5 or 10pm out of season. Apply on arrival.

'**Mission Hotels**' (*missionshotel*) are reasonably priced and popular with Danish family visitors. They are classified as temperance hotels, but will sell wine and beer to guests. There are **motels** around Copenhagen, or you can stay at a nearby village *kro* (**country inn**). These usually small, former stagecoach inns combine good personal service with wholesome food. **Boarding houses** (*pensionat*) and **private rooms** can be booked through the Accommodation Bureau.

You will find that a hearty Danish breakfast is usually included in overnight rates, except at the most expensive hotels.

AIRPORT (*lufthavn*)

Copenhagen Airport, around 10km (6 miles) from the city centre, is one of Europe's busiest. It is also a major gateway to Europe for travellers from the USA, Canada, Japan, Australia and many countries in the Far East and Africa. About 40 airlines have regular flights to and from Copenhagen. Danish domestic flights also link up with destinations in Jutland, as well as with Funen and Bornholm islands, and various domestic flight concessions are made for foreign visitors.

Buses run directly from the airport every 15 minutes to the main railway station in central Copenhagen, a half hour's journey away. Others go to the port of Dragør (south of the airport) for the ferry connection to Limhamn in southern Sweden. A third bus service leaves for the downtown hydrofoil crossing to Malmö.

Copenhagen Airport provides a good shopping centre, with duty-free self-service stores and a variety of boutiques and gift and souvenir shops, including souvenirs from Greenland. There's a bank, post office, nursery, a barber's shop and ladies' hairdresser, shower rooms, rest centre, Danish food shops, restaurant and a large snack-bar area – last chance for a *smørrebrød* and *wienerbrød* feast.

Both porters and luggage trolleys are available. Taxis abound (for fares, see p.131). For **airport information**, ring 31 54 17 01.

Where's the bus for ...?   **Hvorfra afgår bussen til ...?**

B

BABY-SITTERS

Hotel receptionists or the nearest tourist office are likely to know of local baby-sitting services; otherwise you could try the **Students** baby-sitting service (tel. 31 22 96 96); hours are 6.30pm-9am daily except Friday, 3-6pm Monday to Friday and 3-5pm Saturday; but closed on Sundays.

Can you get me a baby-sitter   **Kan De skaffe mig en**
tonight?   **babysitter til i for aften?**   **115**

BICYCLE HIRE (cykeludlejning)

Tourist offices will refer you to local dealers, or, in Copenhagen, you can go direct to **Københavns Cykelbørs** cycle-hire depot at Nørre Farimagsgade 69 (tel. 33 14 07 17). From April to October cycles can also be hired at many railway stations – nearest to Copenhagen are Klampenborg, Lyngby, Hillerød and Helsingør – but advance booking is necessary, so call Central Station on 33 14 17 01. You can return the bike to another railway station in the country, if you prefer, on payment of a nominal freight charge. Organized cycling tours can be arranged through tourist offices in your country or tour operators in Denmark. Routes cover about 40-50km (25-30 miles) a day, and you can choose to stay in a youth hostel, *kro* (inn) or hotel. See the *Cycling Holidays in Denmark* leaflet obtainable free from the **Danish Cyclist Federation** and the Danish Tourist Board. Evidence of identity is always needed when hiring cycles. (**NB** bicycles travel free as 'personal luggage' if you bring your own from home.)

CAMPING (camping)

More than 500 camping sites, eight of them less than 16km (10 miles) from the centre of Copenhagen, are approved by the Camping Council, which means they are frequently visited by health and camping inspectors. The sites range from one- to three-star categories and cover basics from drinking water to provision stores and the services of camp wardens. Unless you have an *International Camping Carnet* you must obtain a Camping Pass for foreigners, valid for the rest of the year, at the first site visited. Camping on private land requires the owner's permission.

You can pick up an excellent free brochure on camping, youth hostels and student hotels from the Danish Tourist Board in your country (see p.135 for addresses). Alternatively, for general information on camping in Denmark, contact Campingrådet, Hesseløgade 16, 2100 Copenhagen Ø; tel. 39 27 88 44.

CAR HIRE (*biludlejning*) (See also DRIVING on p.120 and PLANNING YOUR BUDGET on p.130)

There are several car hire counters at Copenhagen Airport, and the major international agencies are represented in the capital. Tourist information bureaux have lists of local firms. Otherwise, look up under *Autoudlejning* in the trade telephone directory (*Fagbog*).

To hire a car, you'll need a valid national (or international) driving licence and be at least 20 years of age (25 for some firms). It's a good idea to have your passport available, too, although don't leave it with the company. Most agencies will require a cash deposit covering the estimated rental charge; as prices vary considerably, it's worth shopping around. Credit cards are accepted.

CLIMATE and CLOTHING

Denmark's relatively temperate climate is due to its its situation and the sea currents, but frequent switches in the wind also bring changeable weather. Spring may come late, but summer is often sunny and autumn mild. Average monthly temperatures in Copenhagen are:

	J	F	M	A	M	J	J	A	S	O	N	D
temperature °C	0.5	0	2	6	11	16	17	16	13	9	5	2
temperature °F	33	32	35	42	52	60	63	61	56	48	40	36

Clothing. Casual clothes will fit nearly every occasion, including theatre and most dining-out. Only in top-class hotels and clubs will men be required to wear a tie in the evening, and here women will not look out of place in something dressy. Otherwise, go as you like.

Summer nights are long and light but often chilly, so a sweater or cardigan is essential. Bring a light overcoat or raincoat too, in addition to ordinary summer clothes – the weather has an awkward habit of changing. On the beach, you can be as brief as you like.

Spring and autumn have many hours of sunshine, but winter can be downright cold and you should pack plenty of warm clothes (plus a raincoat). In all seasons, comfortable walking shoes are much to be recommended for your tours around the cobbled old-town area.

COMMUNICATIONS (See also OPENING HOURS on p.131 and TIME DIFFERENCES on p.134)

Post offices (*postkontor*). The main post office is at Tietgensgade 35-9 (just behind Tivoli); business hours are Mon-Fri 10am-6pm, Saturday 9am-1pm, closed Sunday. The post office at the Central Station operates longer hours: Mon-Fri 8am-10pm, Saturday 9am-4pm, Sunday 10am-5pm. There are also many sub-offices around town. All display a red sign with a crown, bugle and crossed arrows in yellow – and a sign saying *Kongelig Post og Telegraf*. Stamp machines usually take two 1-krone pieces. When buying postcards from stands and souvenir shops, you can get the appropriate stamps on the spot. Danish postboxes, bright red, stand out cheerfully, as do the postmen – colourful characters in red uniforms riding yellow cycles. You can pick up your **poste restante** (general-delivery) mail at the head post office at Tietgensgade 35-9, postal address: 1704 Copenhagen V) from 9am to 7pm, Monday to Friday, and Saturday from 9am to 1pm, but not on Sunday. Identification is necessary.

Faxes, telex, telegram. Most hotels have fax and telex facilities. The Telecom Centre inside the Central Station on Bernstorffsgade (Mon-Fri 8am-10pm, weekends 9am-9pm; tel. 33 14 20 00) offers services that include fax and telex. All post offices handle telegrams; call 122 (168 for information), or go to the nearest Telecom Centre.

Telephone (*telefon*). Apart from public telephones in newspaper and tobacco kiosks, public boxes are green-painted glass affairs with the word *telefon* on top. Insert 1 krone for short local calls, and 5 krone for long-distance calls. Some telephone booths require the use of a card (a *Telet*), obtainable from kiosks all over town.

For long-distance calls within Denmark, there are no area codes, just dial the 8-digit number of the person you want to call. Beware – telephoning from your hotel room can prove expensive. One of the best places to make long-distance calls is from the Telecom Centre in the railway station.

The main telegraph office at Købmagergade 37 is open for phone calls, telegrams and telex from 9am to 10pm every day.

Some useful numbers:

Telephone operation enquiries:	**141**
Directory enquiries:	**118**
International directory enquiries	**113**

A stamp for this letter/postcard, please.	**Et frimærke til dette brev/postkort, tak.**

CRIME (See also EMERGENCIES on p.124 and POLICE on p.132)

If Copenhagen still counts among the safest capital cities to walk around, things are not all they used to be. Pickpockets are rampant, and petty crime is on the increase. Take normal precautions. Keep a close eye on your belongings. Hesitate before walking out alone in the very early hours through seedy areas – your hotel receptionist can give advice if in doubt about night-time locations you wish to visit. Best to avoid the Christiania area day and night.

CUSTOMS and ENTRY FORMALITIES (*toldkontrol*)

Most visitors – including citizens of the UK, USA, Canada, Eire, Australia and New Zealand – need only to possess a valid passport in order to enter Denmark. British subjects can enter on the simplified Visitor's Passport. You are generally entitled to stay in Denmark for up to three months without a visa. (This period includes the total amount of time spent in Denmark, Finland, Iceland, Norway and Sweden in any six-month period.)

As Denmark belongs to the **European Union (EU)**, free exchange of non-duty free goods for personal use is permitted between Denmark and the UK and Eire. However, duty free items are still subject to restrictions: check before you go.

For residents of **non-EU** countries, restrictions are as follows: **Australia**: 250 cigarettes **or** 250g tobacco; 1l alcohol; **Canada**: 200 cigarettes **and** 50 cigars **and** 400g tobacco; 1.1l spirits **or** wine **or** 8.5l beer; **New Zealand**: 200 cigarettes **or** 50 cigars **or** 250g tobacco; 4.5l wine **or** beer **and** 1.1l spirits; **South Africa**: 400 cigarettes **and** 50 cigars **and** 250g tobacco; 2l wine **and** 1l spirits; **USA**: 200 cigarettes **and** 100 cigars **or** a 'reasonable amount' of tobacco. **119**

Currency restrictions. There is no limit on the amount of Danish or foreign currency that can be brought into or taken out of the country by non-residents. However, anything over 50,000kr can be exported only if it does not exceed the amount originally imported.

D

DISABLED TRAVELLERS

Many institutions in Denmark, as well as the government, pay particular attention to the needs of the disabled. The guide book *Access in Denmark – A Travel Guide for the Disabled* can be obtained from offices of the Danish Tourist Board (see p.135 for addresses). It gives a comprehensive list of accessible areas and facilities for wheelchair users, including public transport, museums and accommodation.

DRIVING IN DENMARK (See also CAR HIRE on p.117)

To take your car into Denmark, you'll need:

- a valid driving licence, showing which type of vehicle it covers
- car registration papers
- Green Card (an extension of your regular insurance policy, valid for travel abroad; though not obligatory for EU countries, it's still preferable to have it)
- a red warning triangle in case of breakdown
- a national identity sticker for your car.

Driving conditions. Drive on the right, pass on the left. Traditionally, traffic coming from your right has priority, but this is decreasingly relevant in Denmark, where most junctions are clearly marked with white broken triangles (called 'sharks' teeth' in Danish), halt signs, traffic lights, etc. Danish national policy is to abolish roundabouts, now considered dangerous because of priority confusion. The Danes are, on the whole, well disciplined drivers and they will expect you to be the same. Clear indication should always be given when changing lanes, either on motorways (expressways) or on the broad thoroughfares that cut through central Copenhagen. Weaving from one lane to another is a punishable offence.

Pedestrian crossings are sacrosanct and nearly always controlled by lights. When turning at lights, you *must* allow pedestrians on the road you are joining to cross first; equally, bikes have priority at any crossing if they want to go straight on when the car turns right.

Beware of buses pulling out from stops – you should give way to them. Caution, also, for cyclists and moped riders to your right, often on their own raised pathways (*cykelsti*), but sometimes divided from you merely by a white line, which you should not cross.

Seat belts must be worn by driver and passengers. Motorcycle, moped and scooter drivers, and their passengers, must wear crash helmets. British car-owners note: left dipping headlights are illegal.

Speed limits. On the *motorvej* (motorway/expressway), the limit is 100kph (68mph). On other roads it is 80kph (50mph) and in built-up areas – indicated by white signs with town silhouettes – it drops to 50kph (30mph). Cars with caravans (trailers) may not exceed 70kph (44mph). If caught speeding, there's a heavy fine – on the spot.

Parking. Traffic wardens in grey uniforms (and police) look for motorists who have parked near signs reading *stopforbudt* (no stopping) or *parkering forbudt* (no parking). They may only put a warning card on your windscreen, but they just might leave a ticket that'll mean a hefty fine. A car that causes a serious obstruction or is double-parked may well be towed away and impounded – and you'll have to pay for the towing, plus a fine. To judge whether you have parked longer than allowed, the warden will look at a disc you should display on your windscreen, indicating the time you arrived. These parking discs (*P-skive* or *parkeringsskive*) can be obtained free from police stations, garages, post offices and most banks.

Stopping and waiting are not allowed within 5m (16ft) of crossroads, pedestrian crossings or exits from cycle tracks. Copenhagen's system of *Datostop* and *Dato-parkering* means that stopping or parking are allowed only on one side of the street – the side of the street with even numbers on even days, the side with odd numbers on odd days. For parking meters you will need 1-, 5- and 10-krone coins. Parked cars should by law always be left locked.

Drinking and driving. The penalties are severe: if you are discovered to have more than 0.8 millilitres of alcohol in your blood while driving, you face a fine equivalent to a month's wages, lose your licence for a year and can be sent to a 'lenient prison'.

Breakdown. If you have a breakdown, you can call FALCK, the breakdown and towing service, in Copenhagen on 33 14 22 22 day and night. Road assistance (only) is given free of charge to members of FIA or AIT motoring organizations. If you aren't a member, you should take out an insurance policy in your home country. Note that a MOMS (VAT/sales tax) of 25% is added to all repair bills.

Fuel and oil (*benzin*; *olie*). Service stations are plentiful, and most international brands of fuel are available, but expensive. However, you can save a few øre per litre at a self-service station (variously called *selvbetjening*, *tank selv* or 'self-service').

Road signs. International pictographs are in widespread use, but here are some written signs you may encounter:

Blind vej	Dead end road (cul-de-sac)
Fare	Danger
Fodgængere	Pedestrians
Indkørsel forbudt	No entry
Omkørsel	Diversion
Rabatten er blød	Soft shoulders
Udkørsel	Exit
Vejarbejde	Roadworks
driving licence	**førerbevis**
car registration papers	**registreringsattest**
green card	**grønt kort**
Can I park here?	**Må jeg parkere her?**
Fill the tank, please …	**Vær venlig at fylde op med …**

normal/super/unleaded	**almindelig/super/blyfri**
Check the oil/tyres/battery, please.	**Vær venlig at kontrollere olien/dækkene/batteriet.**
I've had a breakdown.	**Vognen er gået i stykker.**
There's been an accident.	**Der er sket en ulykke.**

Fluid measures

Distance

E

ELECTRIC CURRENT

The standard voltage is 220, but some camping sites also have 110 available. Note that plugs and sockets in Denmark are different from both British and American types, but if you ask the hotel receptionist you should be able to find an adaptor that you can use.

EMBASSIES and CONSULATES (*ambassade; konsulat*)

Australia: (embassy) Kristianiagade 21,
2100 Copenhagen Ø; tel. 35 26 22 44

Canada: (embassy) Kristen Bernikowsgade 1,
1175 Copenhagen K; tel. 33 12 22 99

Eire: (embassy) Østbanegade 21,
2100 Copenhagen Ø; tel. 31 42 32 33

South Africa: (consulate) Gammel Vartovvej 8,
2900 Hellerup; tel. 31 18 01 55

United Kingdom: (embassy and consulate) Kastelsvej 40, 2100 Copenhagen Ø; tel. 35 26 46 00

USA: (embassy and consulate) Dag Hammarskjölds Allé 24, 2100 Copenhagen Ø; tel. 31 42 31 44

EMERGENCIES

(See also MEDICAL CARE on p.129 and POLICE on p.132)

The all-purpose emergency number is **112**, and is free from public phone boxes. Ask for police, fire or ambulance. Speak distinctly (English will be understood) and state your number and location.

Emergency service (*skadestue*) in central Copenhagen – for accidents only, 24-hours: Kommunehospitalet, Øster Farimagsgade 5, and Rigshospitalet, Blegdamsvej 9 and Tagensvej 20. Medical emergencies in Copenhagen, ring 32 84 00 41 (or 44 53 44 00 if outside the city) 4pm-8am daily and 24 hours at weekends.

Dental emergency. Tandlægevagten, Oslo Plads 14, is open year round, 8am-9.30pm daily, on Saturdays, Sundays and public holidays also 10am to noon, tel. 31 38 02 51. Cash payment only.

ETIQUETTE

The Danes are the most easily approachable as well as the least formal of all Scandinavians, but a handshake on meeting and departure is recognized practice. A pleasantly affable *goddag* ('good day' – pronounced almost as in English) is much appreciated, as is *farvel* ('farewell' or 'goodbye', pronounced far-VELL).

GAY and LESBIAN TRAVELLERS

Denmark has one of Europe's most liberal attitudes towards gays and lesbians, and this is reflected in its legislation. In common with most of Scandinavia, the age of consent is the same as for heterosexuals. Copenhagen has a thriving gay scene, and there are bars, clubs and a few hotels where gays are welcome. For information, contact the Landsforeningen for bøsser og lesbiske (National Organization for Gay Men and Women), Knabrostræde 3; tel. 33 13 19 48.

GUIDES and TOURS (guide)

Sightseeing tour buses and some canal boats will be accompanied by a multilingual guide. Contact the tourist office on 33 11 13 25 for details of authorized guides, or consult the listings in *Copenhagen This Week*. Your hotel will also have information on tour programmes.

Brewery visits. A brewery tour is an excellent way to spend time, not only to sample a free bottle or two, but also to discover how every glass you drink is a contribution to art, science or industry: Carlsberg and Tuborg donate vast sums through their charitable foundations. **Carlsberg** (tel. 33 27 13 14) is at the Elephant Gate, Ny Carlsbergvej 140 (bus 6 from Rådhuspladsen); guided tours in several languages at 11am and 2pm. **Tuborg** (tel. 33 27 22 12) is at Strandvejen 54, Hellerup (bus 1 from Rådhuspladsen); tours for groups only until the end of 1995, and thereafter no tours at all.

Canal and harbour tours. Though the city hasn't as extensive a network of waterways as Venice or Amsterdam, Copenhagen's canals offer a delightful 50-minute trip on a fine day. Gammel Strand and Nyhavn (at Kongens Nytorv) are the two main starting points. From May to October, 90-minute waterbus tours – some with guided commentary – give you an excellent view of the inner city and harbour.

City tours. Copenhagen Excursions and Vikingbus operate organized **bus tours** covering the major sights; duration from 1½ to 2¾ hours. The **Royal Tour** includes a visit to the Reception Chambers at Christiansborg Palace and the crown jewels at Rosenborg, while the **Grand Tour** aims to give visitors an overall impression of the city, ending with attendance at the changing of the guard ceremony at Amalienborg Palace. There are also guided **walking tours** of Copenhagen several times weekly during the summer, with an English-speaking guide. Guided **tours by bike** operate between June and October. Other tours run by taxi, limousine and sightseeing flights.

Industrial art tours. There are guided tours in English of the Royal Copenhagen **porcelain** factory, Smallegade 45, between June and

September Monday to Friday at 9am, 10am and 11am, also at 1pm and 2pm in the summer. Similar tours run to **silver** and **glass** works.

Themed tours. Choose between a leisurely afternoon **Hamlet** tour or a full day's trip to North Zealand's **castles**. Also a 6hr **Vikingland** tour (Roskilde cathedral and the Viking Ship Museum), an 11hr trip to **Hans Christian Andersen**'s home town of Odense on the island of Funen, and a 13hr tour to **Legoland** (advance booking essential).

Trips to Sweden. Sweden is so close and accessible that it really is worth the short trip – if only to see how Swedes differ from Danes.

From Havnegade, Nyhavn, in the centre of Copenhagen, two companies – Flyvebådene and Pilen – offer a 45-minute catamaran service right into the heart of Malmö. An alternative is to combine a trip to Helsingør with the 20-minute ferry boat service to Helsingborg.

The more adventurous can try a 'Round the Sound' trip. Buy your tickets from *DBS* (Danish State Railways) and travel, in either direction, from Copenhagen to Malmö, up to Helsingborg by train, across the sound to Helsingør and back to Copenhagen by train.

L

LANGUAGE (See also the USEFUL EXPRESSIONS on the cover)

English is very widely spoken and understood. Danish is perhaps the most difficult northern European language for relating the written word to speech; it's almost impossible to pronounce simply by reading the words, as many syllables are swallowed rather than spoken. Thus the island of Amager becomes *Am-air,* with the 'g' disappearing, but in a distinctive Danish way difficult for the visitor to imitate. The letter 'd' becomes something like a 'th', but with the tongue placed behind the lower teeth, not the upper. The letter 'ø' is like the 'u' in English n**u**rse, but spoken with the lips far forward. And the letter 'r' is again swallowed.

There are 29 letters in the Danish alphabet – the 26 'normal', plus 'æ' (as in **e**gg), 'ø', and 'å' (as in p**o**rt). They appear *after* the usual 26 (a point to note when looking up names in phone books and lists).

DAYS

Monday	**mandag**	Friday	**fredag**
Tuesday	**tirsdag**	Saturday	**lørdag**
Wednesday	**onsdag**	Sunday	**søndag**
Thursday	**torsdag**		

MONTHS

January	**januar**	July	**juli**
February	**februar**	August	**august**
March	**marts**	September	**september**
April	**april**	October	**oktober**
May	**maj**	November	**november**
June	**juni**	December	**december**

NUMBERS

0	**nul**	10	**ti**	20	**tyve**
1	**en**	11	**elleve**	30	**tredive**
2	**to**	12	**tolv**	40	**fyrre**
3	**tre**	13	**tretten**	50	**halvtreds**
4	**fire**	14	**fjorten**	60	**tres**
5	**fem**	15	**femten**	70	**halvfjerds**
6	**seks**	16	**seksten**	80	**firs**
7	**syv**	17	**sytten**	90	**halvfems**
8	**otte**	18	**atten**	100	**hundrede**
9	**ni**	19	**nitten**	1000	**tusind**

The Berlitz DANISH PHRASE BOOK AND DICTIONARY covers practically all situations you're likely to encounter in your travels in Denmark, and the DANISH-ENGLISH/ENGLISH-DANISH pocket dictionary contains some 12,500 concepts, and a special menu-reader supplement, that will help tackle the worst stumbling blocks.

LAUNDRY and DRY CLEANING (*vask; kemisk rensning*)

The large hotels offer same-day service, but not on weekends and holidays – and it's expensive. Dry cleaners are found throughout the city and are entered in the directory (*Fagbog*) under *Renserier*. Prices in launderettes (*selvbetjeningsvaskeri*) are lower, and these are open till late at night.

When will it be ready? **Hvornår er det færdigt?**

I must have this for **Jeg skal bruge det i**
tomorrow morning. **morgen tidlig.**

LOST PROPERTY (*hittegods*)

The **general** lost-property office (*hittegodskontor*) is at the police station at Slotsherrensvej 113, Vanløse (tel. 31 74 88 22), open Mon-Fri 9am-2pm (Thursday till 5pm), closed Saturday and Sunday. For property lost in **buses** or **trains**, the address to contact is Lyshøjgårdsvej 80, Valby; for buses tel. 36 45 45 45 then dial 4 Mon-Fri 10am-5pm; for trains tel. 36 44 20 10 Mon-Fri 9am-4pm. For missing **credit cards** call Eurocard Denmark, tel. 44 89 25 00 (24hrs) or, for American Express cardholders, tel. 80 01 00 21.

MEDIA

Newspapers and magazines (*avis; ugeblad*). You'll have no problem finding English-language newspapers and magazines at newsstands, shops and hotels throughout central Copenhagen. The kiosk at the Central Station sells foreign-language publications, and you'll find a good selection at Magasin du Nord (Kongens Nytorv 13) and Illums (52-54 Østergade) department stores. There is also a free monthly English-language brochure, *Copenhagen This Week*, which lists comprehensive information for visitors.

Radio and TV (*radio; fjernsyn*). Danish radio has three channels – Radio 1 (on 90.8 MHz VHF) for news and comment and classical music, and channels 2 and 3 (96.5/93.9 MHz) for local news, lighter music and entertainment. There's a news programme in English on Radio 3 at 8.30am, Monday to Friday. BBC long-wave and world services, and European-based American networks can be picked up.

The main television transmission is from 7.30am to 11.30pm. All films are shown in their original version with Danish subtitles.

Have you any English-language newspapers?	**Har De engelsksprogede aviser?**

MEDICAL CARE (See also EMERGENCIES on p.124)

Make sure your health insurance covers any illness or accident while on holiday. Your travel agent or insurance company will advise you.

In Denmark, treatment and even hospitalization is free for any tourist taken suddenly ill or involved in an accident. For minor treatments, doctors, dentists and chemists will charge on the spot. For EU employees or pensioners and their families, however, this money will be partly refunded at the local Danish health service office on production of bills and the EU form E111. It's wise to ask before you go about possible reciprocal health agreements and any forms needed.

A Danish **chemist/pharmacy** (*apotek*) is strictly a dispensary. Some medicines which can be bought over the counter in other countries are available only on prescription. Pharmacies are listed in the trade phone book under *Apoteker*. Normal hours are from 9am to 5.30pm and until 1pm on Saturday. An all-night service operates at Steno Apotek, Vesterbrogade 6C; tel. 33 14 82 66.

I need a doctor/dentist.	**Jeg har brug for en læge/tandlæge.**

MONEY MATTERS

(See also CUSTOMS and ENTRY FORMALITIES on p.119)

Currency. The unit of Danish currency is the *krone*, abbreviated *kr*, or, abroad, Dkr (to distinguish it from the Norwegian and Swedish krone). It is divided into 100 *øre*.

Coins: 25 and 50 *øre*; 1, 2, 5, 10 and 20 *kroner*.

Banknotes: 50, 100, 500 and 1,000 *kroner*.

Banks and currency-exchange offices (*bank; vekselkontor*). Banks and bureaux de change offer the best exchange rates for foreign cash. You pay a flat commission per transaction at banks, which are open Mon-Fri 9.30am-4pm (6pm on Thursday). Outside banking hours, exchange bureaux operate at the Central Station every day of the week from 6.45am to 10pm and at the entrance to Tivoli in HC Andersens Boulevard from noon to 11pm during the high season (May to mid-September). Exchange bureaux also sell *Copenhagen Cards*, stamps, bus and train tickets.

Credit cards and traveller's cheques (*kreditkort; rejsecheck*). Major hotels and many restaurants – and some tourist shops, too – will accept payment by international credit cards. There's little problem with traveller's cheques, provided you bring along passport identification. Both traveller's cheques and Eurocheques can also be cashed at banks in Denmark.

MOMS. Danish VAT (sales tax) is called MOMS and is set at 25%. It's always included in the bill. For expensive purchases (over 600kr), there are special tax-free export schemes. Look out for shops displaying the signs Europe Tax-Free Shopping or Tax-Free International; retailers are well acquainted with the necessary procedures.

PLANNING YOUR BUDGET

The following are some average prices in Danish kroner (kr) for basic expenses. However, remember that all prices must be regarded as *approximate*. Danes round off the bill, up or down, to the closest amount possible divisible by 25 øre because there are no intermediate coins (e.g. 13 is rounded off to 25).

Airport transfer. Bus to Rådhuspladsen 15kr. Special airport bus directly to Central Station 30kr; taxi 140kr (tip included).

Baby-sitters. 25kr per hour. Booking fee 25kr, including transport.

Bicycle hire. 50kr a day, 225kr a week, deposit 200kr.

Camping. Camping pass for foreign visitors 24 kr per person per night, children half price.

Car hire. *Ford Escort* 1.3 680kr per day, 3,010kr per week; *Volvo 740* (station wagon) 1,050kr per day, 4,690kr per week; *Audi 100* (automatic) 1,100kr per day, 5,460kr per week; all prices include unlimited mileage, but exclude insurance. Add 25% tax.

Copenhagen Card. One day 140kr, two days 230kr, three days 295kr. Half price for children under 12.

Entertainment. Cinema 55kr, Royal Ballet tickets 40-300kr, nightclub entry 30-60kr. Tivoli: adults 38kr, children half price.

Hotels. Top class 1,000-1,800kr, medium 600-800kr, inexpensive 400-600kr for double room with bathroom and breakfast.

Meals and drinks (at a fairly good establishment). Lunch 70kr, dinner 150kr, sandwich (*smørrebrød*) 15-20kr, coffee 12kr, akvavit (*schnaps*) 25kr, beer 25kr, soft drink 15kr.

Public transport. Flat-rate ticket (*grundbillet*) for single bus ride or S-train ride 9kr. Ticket coupons (*rabatkort*) for 10 rides: blue 70kr, yellow 80kr, lilac 150kr, grey 215kr.

Shopping bag. Bread 10kr, 250g of butter 10kr, 6 eggs 10kr, ½kg of beefsteak (choice meat) 35kr, 500g of instant coffee 25kr, bottle of beer 3.75kr, soft drink 4kr.

Taxi. Meter charge 12kr; 8kr per km between 6am and 6pm, 10kr per km between 6pm and 6am and at weekends.

OPENING HOURS

Banks are open Monday-Friday 9.30am-4pm, Thursday until 6pm. In the provinces, hours fluctuate from town to town.

Post offices are open 9 or 10am-5 or 5.30pm during the week; some post offices also open on Saturday 9am-noon.

Shops and **department stores** are open Monday-Friday 9.30 or 10am-5.30pm. Late-night shopping on Friday to 7pm. Some are closed on Monday or Tuesday. Saturday hours are 9am-noon or 2pm, except for the first Saturday in the month when they close at 5pm.

There are no regularized hours for **museums** in Copenhagen, and times are subject to frequent change. The most likely closing day is Monday, and shorter hours generally operate during the winter.

PHOTOGRAPHY

Film is relatively inexpensive, so it's not worth bringing a stock from home. Developing and printing are of a high quality and can be done quickly in the centre; try **Express Foto**, Axeltorv 2, tel. 33 15 27 80.

For detailed information on how to get the most out of your holiday photographs, purchase a copy of the Berlitz–Nikon GUIDE TO TRAVEL PHOTOGRAPHY (available in the UK only).

I'd like a film for this camera.	**Jeg vil gerne have en film til dette apparat.**
a black-and-white film	**en sort-hvid film**
colour prints	**en farvefilm**
colour slides	**en film til lysbilleder**
How long will it take to develop (and print) this film?	**Hvor lang tid tager det at fremkalde (og kopiere) denne film?**
May I take a picture?	**Må jeg tage et billede?**

POLICE (See also EMERGENCIES on p.124)

State and city police all form part of the national force and are dressed in black uniforms. Some walk their beat through central Copenhagen, but most policemen patrol in deep-blue-and-white or white cars with the word *POLITI* in large letters (although they also tend to roam around in unmarked cars). You're entitled to stop police cars at any time and request help. Police are courteous and speak English (they take a mandatory 80 English lessons during training).

Don't hesitate to go to the local police station if in need of advice. All are listed in the phone book under *Politi*.

Where's the nearest police station?	**Hvor er den nærmeste politi-station?**

PUBLIC HOLIDAYS *(fest-/helligdag)*

Though Denmark's banks, offices and major shops close on public holidays, museums and tourist attractions will be open, if on reduced hours. It will also be business as usual in the cafés.

1 January	*Nytår*	New Year's Day
5 June (half-day)	*Grundslovsdag*	Constitution Day
25/26 December	*Jul*	Christmas
Movable dates:	*Skærtorsdag*	Maundy Thursday
	Langfredag	Good Friday
	Anden påskedag	Easter Monday
	Bededag	General Prayer Day (fourth Friday after Easter)
	Kristi himmelfartsdag	Ascencion Day
	Anden pinsedag	Whit Monday

Are you open tomorrow? **Har De åbent i morgen?**

R

RELIGIOUS SERVICES

The Danish Church is Protestant (Evangelical Lutheran). Sunday services in English are held in the following places of worship:

Church of England. St Alban's Anglican Episcopalian Church, Churchillparken, Langelinie. Morning services, Holy Communion.

The American Church of Copenhagen. Interdenominational and International, Farvergade 27. Services every Sunday morning, followed by Coffee Fellowship.

Roman Catholic. Jesu Hjerte Kirke, Stenosgade 4. Morning mass.

Jewish services are held in Hebrew in the Synagogue, Krystalgade 12, daily in the early morning and evening.

133

TIME DIFFERENCES

Denmark sticks to Central European Time (GMT + 1) along with most of the Continent. In summer, the clock is put one hour ahead (GMT + 2), and the time differences look like this:

New York	London	**Copenhagen**	Jo'burg	Sydney	Auckland
7am	noon	**1pm**	1pm	9pm	11pm

What time is it, please?   **Undskyld, hvad er klokken?**

TIPPING

This is a non-existent problem since basically you don't give tips. Hotel and restaurant bills always include service; tip only if special services have been rendered. Railway porters charge fixed prices, and no need to tip hairdressers, taxi drivers, theatre or cinema ushers. Only in a very few cases is there an exception to the rule, as for instance, when you leave the odd krone tip for use of the washbasin and facilities in toilets.

TOILETS/RESTROOMS

Facilities are usually indicated by a pictograph; alternatively they are marked *WC*, *Toiletter*, *Damer/Herrer* (Ladies/Gentlemen) or just by *D/H*. There's no charge unless you see it clearly marked otherwise.

Where are the toilets?   **Hvor er toilettet?**

TOURIST INFORMATION OFFICES (*turistinformation*)

Danish tourist offices are often very helpful, and can provide copious information and a range of first-class brochures.

Australia: Danish Tourist Board, 60 Market Street, PO Box 4531, Melbourne, Victoria 3001.

Canada: Danish Tourist Board, PO Box 115, Station 'N', Toronto, Ontario M8V 3S4.

United Kingdom: Danish Tourist Board,
169-173 Regent Street, London W1R 8PY;
tel. (0171) 734-2637/8.

USA: Scandinavian National Tourist Offices,
655 Third Avenue, 18th floor, New York,
NY 10017; tel. (212) 949-2333.

Scandinavian Tourist Board, Denmark-Sweden,
150 North Michigan Avenue, Suite 2110,
Chicago, IL 60601; tel. (312) 899-1121.

Scandinavian Tourist Board, Denmark-Sweden,
8929 Wilshire Boulevard, Suite 300,
Beverly Hills, CA 90211; tel. (213) 854-1549.

All Danish cities and most small towns have their own tourist information office marked by a large letter **i** on a green background. The main information office is near Tivoli at Bernstorffsgade 1, tel. 33 11 13 25, open daily 9am-8pm during the summer; winter Monday-Friday 9am-5pm, Saturday 9am-2pm, closed Sunday.

Where's the tourist office? **Hvor ligger turistbureauet?**

TRANSPORT

Bus and S-Train. An excellent public transport system of frequent buses (*bus*) and electrified trains (*S-tog*) starts weekdays at 5am and Sunday at 6am. The last main services leave the centre at 12.30am, although there are several all-night buses (*natbusser*). For bus information, call 36 45 45 45 then dial 3 for personal service (7am-11pm); for S-train information, tel. 33 14 17 01 (Central Station).

Tickets. The fare system in Copenhagen is somewhat complicated. It is valid for the HT-area – the city and surrounding region of 40km (24 miles) – which has been split into zones. Tickets entitle you to travel and transfer within a zone and to bordering zones for a limited period of time. Tickets are interchangeable on buses and trains, which begin like an underground railway in the central district and then emerge into daylight on the suburban network.

135

Purchase a flat fare ticket (*grundbillet*) for single rides within a zone and to bordering zones only. Additional tickets, available at an extra cost, are required if you travel beyond the basic ticket zone. The more advantageous ticket coupons (*rabatkort*) are valid for 10 rides in several zones. Blue coupons are good for 2 zones, yellow for 3 zones, lilac for 5 zones and grey for all zones. They can be purchased at train stations or from bus drivers.

Enter by the front door, tell the driver your destination and you'll be given the right ticket. Don't forget to time-stamp your coupon (face up) aboard the bus or in the yellow, automatic machines on train platforms. Passengers without valid stamped tickets are liable to on-the-spot fines. Children under 6 travel free, ages 6-12 half-fare.

Car Ferries. Since Denmark is largely an archipelago, it's hardly surprising that car ferries are a familiar feature of the country's everyday life. Though spectacular bridges have been built linking some of the islands, a good many places can still only be reached by boat. You certainly won't be disappointed in the regular, efficient ferry services that conveniently cover the islands and the Jutland peninsula. All the major routes carry both cars and passengers. Detailed timetables including rates and conditions are available from the Danish National Tourist Board, in English. Fares vary according to the weight and length of the car; prices quoted may include passengers, so check beforehand. It's highly advisable to book a day ahead, at least for domestic crossings – the Danes do, especially in summer when boats tend to be quite full. Be in good time (30 minutes) for embarkation, or you'll probably lose your reservation.

Taxi. Plenty of taxis cruise the streets of Copenhagen, but in wet weather it's difficult to find a vacant one. They are recognized by a *Taxi* or *Taxa* sign. Tips are included in the meter price, but round the sum off upwards – if pleased with service. All cabs are radio-controlled; call 31 35 35 35 or 31 35 14 20 – or for a mini-bus taxi, 31 39 35 35. Most drivers speak English.

Copenhagen with its suburbs extends for miles, so have a look at where your destination lies and check on the availability of the cheaper bus or train services before leaping into a cab.

Trains (*tog*). A comprehensive and punctual network dealing with 1,200 movements a day operates from Copenhagen Central Station.

Regional or coast diesel trains (*Kystbanerne*) cover outer Zealand.

Intercity trains (*Intercity*) are the backbone of Danish State Railways' (*DSB-Danske Statsbaner*) long-distance traffic. For instance, one leaves every hour for Jutland; the whole train is shunted aboard the Great Belt ferry to Funen island (seat reservations are required for through-passengers; ring the Central Station on 33 14 17 01).

Long-distance trains (*Lyntog*), 'ultra-specials' reaching 140kph (87mph), also run to Jutland and, like intercity trains, have buffet bars, plus phones for passengers' use (seat reservations are required).

International trains, usually referred to by name (e.g. *Vikingen* or *Øresundspilen* for Stockholm), link Copenhagen with most of Europe. They have sleeping cars and couchette coaches for night travel.

Copenhagen card. Similar to a plastic credit card, this discount tourist card offers unlimited travel on buses and trains in metropolitan Copenhagen, free entrance to many of the major museums and sights and up to 50 per cent discount on ferry routes connecting Zealand with Sweden and on hydrofoils between Copenhagen and Malmö. The card is valid for one, two or three days and is on sale at tourist information offices (see p.1350 for addresses), travel agencies, currency-exchange bureaux, all main railway stations in Denmark, and at certain Copenhagen hotels.

TRAVELLING TO COPENHAGEN (See AIRPORT on p.115)

If the choice of ways to go is bewildering, the complexity of fares and regulations can be downright stupefying. A reliable travel agent will have full details of all the latest flights, fares and regulations.

By Air. Copenhagen Airport is on several intercontinental routes – mainly from North America and the Middle and Far East. There are frequent regional services from most European cities. Average journey time London-Copenhagen is 1 hour and 45 minutes, New York-Copenhagen 7 hours and 40 minutes. From the UK an alternative service is run by AIR UK from the less congested Stansted airport, accessible from Liverpool Street Station via the Stansted Express. **137**

By Rail/Sea/Car. Ferry services to Denmark are generally into Esbjerg (from the UK), to Gedser (from Germany) and to numerous ports (including Copenhagen itself) for travellers arriving from Norway and Sweden.

Inter-Rail and *Eurail* cards are valid on all routes into Denmark.

There are road and rail links into Jutland from Schleswig-Holstein in Germany, and through-trains from Hamburg to Copenhagen.

WATER (*vand*)
You can drink water without any qualms from the tap in Denmark. Home-produced mineral water, if you prefer it, is excellent.

A glass of water, please. **Et glas vand, tak.**

WEIGHTS and MEASURES
For fluid and distance, see p.123. Denmark uses the metric system.

Length

Weight

Temperature

WOMEN TRAVELLERS

Women can wander almost anywhere in Copenhagen without being subjected to sexual harassment. As in most cities around the world, however, it is prudent to avoid travelling alone late at night on the underground and to keep away from the red light area that centres around the railway station.

A couple of useful organizations are:

American Women's Club in Denmark, PO Box 34, 2800 Lyngby.

International Women's Group, tel. 44 98 55 59.

YOUTH HOSTELS (*vandrerhjem*)

Copenhagen is something of a mecca for rucksack travellers. There are nine city youth hostels and student hotels to cater for the influx and to prevent sleeping rough in the parks, which is frowned upon. Youth hostels as such require a membership card issued by an organization affiliated to the International Youth Hostel Association. If you haven't got such a card, you can obtain a guest card from Denmark's Youth Hostels (address below).

Bed linen can be hired at the hostel (down bags are not permitted). There's no age limit. A full list of Denmark's 80 odd youth hostels is available on request from Danish Tourist Board offices abroad.

Danmarks Vandrerhjem (Denmark's Youth Hostels), Vesterbrogade 39, 1620 Copenhagen V; tel. 31 31 36 12. Open Mon-Thurs 9am-4pm, Friday until 3pm. April-August Thursday 9am-6pm.

At a student hotel (*ungdomsherberg*), restrictions on night-time closure and other practises are more relaxed.

For any information specifically in the youth field, call in at **Huset** ('Use It') downtown youth information centre (see p.25) at Rådhusstræde 13 (tel. 33 15 65 18), open daily 9am-10pm. At other times a noticeboard indicates room availability.

Index

Where there is more than one set of references, the one in **bold** refers to the main entry. Page numbers in *italic* refer to an illustration.

141

SUZA

non
the
trav
A

19.6.21

Please return/renew this item by the last date shown.
Items may also be renewed by the internet*

https://library.eastriding.gov.uk

* Please note a PIN will be required to access this service
- this can be obtained from your library